REVISED AND UPDATED

CW00500048

THE HARDY WAY
A 19TH-CENTURY PILGRIMAGE

MARGARET MARANDE

BLUE BIRCH
DORSET

TO LIZ
WITH LOVE AND GRATITUDE

Copyright © 2015 Margaret Marande

The right of Margaret Marande to be identified as the Author of the Work has been asserted by her in accordance with the Copyright, Designs and Patents Act 1988.

First published in 1995 by Dorset Publishing Company

This second edition published in 2015 by Blue Birch, Dorset

Maps courtesy of ©OpenStreetMap (www.openstreetmap.org/copyright) adapted by Ben Pyrke to show Thomas Hardy locations. Original maps based upon Ordnance Survey first editions, reprinted with some addditions from 1811, now out of copyright. Illustrations collected by the late Rodney Legg. All rights reserved.

No part of this publication may be reproduced, stored in a retrieval system, or transmitted in any form or by any means, electronic, computerised, recorded, photocopied or otherwise, without prior permission in writing from the publisher.

Cataloguing in Publication Data is available from the British Library

ISBN 978-0-9931628-0-0

Designed by Fiona Pike, Pike Design

Printed by Printondemand-worldwide

Published by Blue Birch, Dorset
37 South Street,
Fontmell Magna,
Shaftesbury,
Dorset SP7 0PD

CONTENTS

What was said about the first edition of THE HARDY WAY:

'the book plunges into *Thomas Hardy country ... is stuffed with poems, extracts from Hardy's works and contemporary photographs*'
Hester Lacey, *Independent on Sunday*

'A unique guide ... walking back in time as well as forward along the route'
Linda Hart in *The Great Outdoors* magazine

'Can't praise the guidebook highly enough'
Vincent Crump, in *Country Walking* magazine

'A joy for ramblers and Hardy fans'
Western Gazette

'refreshingly different ... a terrific book'
Southern Echo

'a wealth of knowledge on history, wildlife, landscapes and most of all Hardy's literature'
Dorset, the Magazine for *People Who like to Explore*

'Margaret Marande's book overflows with details of Thomas Hardy and his works, of the Wessex he knew then and the Dorset you will see now'
Rambling Today magazine

'A great achievement! Margaret Marande and Dorset County Council are to be congratulated on this wonderful walk'
British Epilepsy Association

'Enjoyable walking with a real sense of purpose'
Ann Bird, in *Global Adventure* magazine

'Beautiful countryside and historic places ... stunningly drawn pictures'
Bridport and Lyme Regis News

INTRODUCTION

I am delighted to be writing this introduction to the second edition of *The Hardy Way* which has become necessary partly because the first edition is out of print and also because so much has changed on the ground since 1995 that revision is urgently required!

Thomas Hardy's descriptions of nineteenth century rural 'Wessex' and its people are so evocative that they engender nostalgia for a time when life was lived at a slower pace and man not besieged by the problems of global pollution, especially those caused by motor transport. In reality conditions were often far from idyllic and in his novels Hardy, like Dickens, exposed injustices that caused hardship. Today, in spite of 'progress', there are still places in the Wessex countryside that remain tranquil and unspoiled but which are now happily free of the extreme poverty experienced by many in Hardy's day.

The aim of this book is to lead the walker and those who enjoy Hardy's work on a trail through Wessex, over an area extending from Shaftesbury in north Dorset to the Isle of Portland in the south and from Cranborne Chase in the east to Beaminster in the west. The Hardy Way can be walked as a circular long distance walk of about two hundred and twenty miles or in shorter sections using public transport wherever possible. I have described the walk as a pilgrimage for two reasons. Firstly because it is a long journey that passes many locations held sacred by Hardy admirers and, secondly, because it ends as all true pilgrimages do, in a holy place – Stinsford churchyard – where his heart is buried.

The walk directions and points of factual interest are on the right-hand pages: the fictional references and extracts from Hardy's work are on facing left-hand pages closely linked with the walk for facility of use. There is sometimes a very fine distinction between fiction and reality and, of course, opinions vary about exact imagined locations. Generally I have preferred to ignore the phrase 'may have been' and I ask the reader to accept that the parallels I have chosen are open to discussion.

I have used maps created by OpenStreetMap adding Hardy locations where necessary. Some of these maps also show cycle routes in a thick line. I have also retained a couple of the 1811 Ordnance Survey maps that were in the first edition to give a flavour of the nineteenth century. These were not easy to follow. The OpenStreetMaps will be more helpful but it would also be good to supplement them with Modern O.S. Explorer maps OL 15, 118, 129,117 (in order of use). To the best of my knowledge the walk is entirely on existing rights of way, permissive paths or over ground where access is traditionally free for all.

I hope the Hardy Way will give as much pleasure to those who walk it as it has given me creating it.

ACKNOWLEDGEMENTS

The late Rodney Legg enabled me to produce the first edition of *The Hardy Way* and gave me an enormous amount of help with the illustrations. Stella Cork drew the original map of the route.

Dorset County Council Rights of Way Department, in particular Lisa Dover, and the Ramblers' Association were responsible for waymarking the route. The Thomas Hardy Society gave generous support, especially Dr Geoffrey Tapper, who organised the official opening of the Way at Max Gate in 1998 by kind permission of Andrew and Marilyn Leah the then National Trust tenants. Andrew, and Sue Clarke of the THS, have also shown interest in this new edition, Andrew in particular detailing the route on OS maps which has been very useful.

I am indebted to Arthur Simmonds of Shaftesbury who has given invaluable help in checking and updating the route with many practical suggestions for utilising public transport. This information will be available in a leaflet from the publisher. I am also very grateful to Dr Robin Peel of Plymouth University for his enlightening and invaluable reports of walking the whole route which I found most helpful in making my own revision. Helen Lane has walked much of the route with me. My grandson, Ben Pyrke, has also walked and has been a tower of strength in the reproduction of the new maps; his computer expertise has made a huge difference! I would also like to thank my family, especially Harry Holberry, for their interest and patience with me for spending a lot of time on this project.

THE HARDY WAY starts at Hardy's birthplace, Higher Bockhampton, near Dorchester. It traverses a large area of Dorset, of which over fifty miles is spectacular coastal scenery. At its most northerly point, near Shaftesbury, the Way enters Wiltshire for a few miles. There is plenty of accommodation along the route.

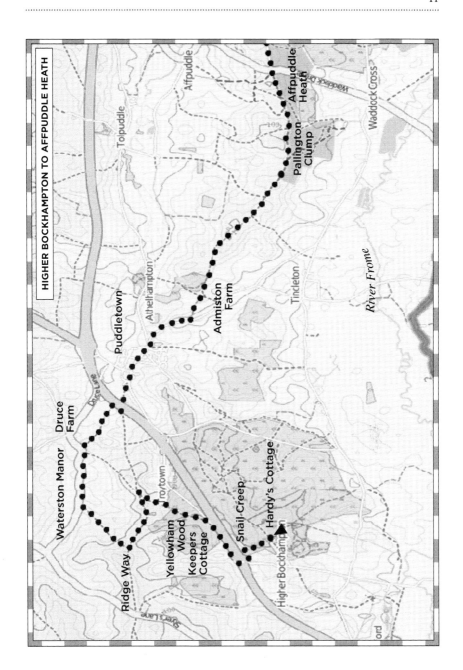

HIGHER BOCKHAMPTON/UPPER MELLSTOCK

The earliest known of Hardy's poems, written when he was in his late teens, is
Domicilium:

It faces west, and round the back and sides
High beeches bending, hang a veil of boughs,
And sweep against the roof. Wild honeysucks
Climb on the walls, and seem to sprout a wish
(If we may fancy wish of trees and plants)
To overtop the apple-trees hard by.

Red roses, lilacs, variegated box
Are there in plenty, and such hardy flowers
As flourish best untrained. Adjoining these
Are herbs and esculents; and farther still
A field; then cottages with trees, and last
The distant hills and sky.

Behind, the scene is wilder. Heath and furze
Are everything that seems to grow and thrive
Upon the uneven ground. A stunted thorn
Stands here and there, indeed; and from a pit
An oak uprises, springing from a seed
Dropped by some bird a hundred years ago.

In days bygone-
Long gone – my father's mother, who is now
Blest with the blest, would take me out to walk.
At such a time I once inquired of her
How looked the spot when first she settled here.
The answer I remember. 'Fifty years
Have passed since then, my child, and change has marked
The face of all things. Yonder garden-plots
And orchards were uncultivated slopes
O'ergrown with bramble bushes, furze and thorn:
That road a narrow path shut in by ferns,
Which, almost trees, obscured the passer-by.

THE BIRTHPLACE AT HIGHER BOCKHAMPTON TO WOOL

This is where it began — in a thatched cottage two miles from Dorchester. Here, on 2 June 1840, a baby was born so puny that he was almost thrown aside as dead. But Thomas Hardy lived to be eighty-seven and became one of England's greatest writers. He lived here for most of his first twenty-two years before going to train and work as an architect in London, after which he often returned to revitalise and to write until his marriage in 1874. From the bedroom behind the right-hand dormer window came four novels including *Under The Greenwood Tree* and *Far From The Madding Crowd*.

Hardy's paternal great grandfather, a mason and bricklayer, built the cottage in 1800. The leasehold expired when Hardy's father, also Thomas, died in 1892 but the family continued to rent the cottage from the nearby **Kingston Maurward** estate until 1913. Hardy always retained an affection for his birthplace. He recalled that his grandfather had engaged in smuggling, a common practice amongst country folk in the area in the eighteenth and nineteenth centuries. Sometimes up to eight barrels of brandy were stored here; the smugglers' signal being a whiplash on the window in the night. Hardy's grandmother put a stop to this!

Since 1948 the National Trust has owned and administered the property. It is currently open from mid March until about the end of October, Wednesdays to Sundays and on Bank Holidays, 11a.m. to 5p.m. — last entries 4.30p.m. Group bookings: Tel. 01297 489481. A new Visitor Centre, with café and toilets is near the Car Park, open all year round from 10a.m. to 4p.m. Tel. 01305 251228.

In 1840 heathland backed **Higher Bockhampton**; today forestry plantations engulf most of the 'Egdon Heath' that Hardy loved.

The Hardy Way begins behind the cottage at the monument erected in 1931 by American admirers. Take the path signposted northward to the A35. This is **The Snail Creep**. Follow uphill through a wood (mainly beech) and where the path forks keep straight on the main path down to join the

'Our house stood quite alone, and those tall firs
And beeches were not planted. Snakes and efts
Swarmed in the summer days, and nightly bats
Would fly about our bedrooms. Heathcroppers
Lived on the hills, and were our friends;
So wild it was when first we settled here.'

Heathcroppers were the small, hardy ponies which eked a living on the heath;
they were similar to New Forest ponies.

Hardy's cottage is the Dewy's cottage in *Under the Greenwood Tree:*

It was a long low cottage with a hipped roof of thatch, having dormer windows
breaking up into the eaves, a chimney standing in the middle of the ridge and
another at each end ... The walls of the dwelling were for the most part covered
with creepers, though these were rather beaten back from the doorway – a
feature which was worn and scratched by much passing in and out, giving
it by day the appearance of an old keyhole.

THE SNAIL CREEP

This is the path Dick Dewy took from his home at **Upper Mellstock** to go nutting
with his sweetheart Fancy Day in **Grey's Wood**, just west of Yalbury Wood in
Under the Greenwood Tree. In the event Dick went alone without the capricious
Fancy – a girl most certainly too anxious about her frocks.

YELLOWHAM WOOD/YALBURY WOOD

Yalbury Wood was owned by the Earl of Wessex in *Under the Greenwood Tree.*
Fancy Day's father Geoffrey, the head gamekeeper, timber steward and general
overlooker for this district lived in a cottage there with his wife and daughter:

A curl of wood-smoke came from the chimney and drooped over the roof like a
blue feather in a lady's hat ...

In *Far from the Madding Crowd* the shepherd Gabriel Oak passed through
Yalbury Wood looking for work:

... where the game-birds were rising to their roosts, ... heard the crack-voiced
cock-pheasants' 'cu-uck, cuck,' and the wheezy whistle of the hens.

road. This is a complete contrast to the tranquillity of Higher Bockhampton but the bridge has to be crossed to get to **Yellowham Wood**. In 1901, before the days of motor traffic, Jemima, Hardy's aged mother, watched from the roadside in her wheelchair as eminent visitors passed in open carriages to visit her famous son at **Max Gate**, his Dorchester home.

Over the bridge join the old main road parallel to the A35 north-east past Yellowham Farm entrance then on for about a quarter of a mile after a farm machinery depot to take a signposted track off to the left. This soon passes the smallholding of **Keeper's Cottage**, its front windows with leaded diamond glazing. In 2015 the tenant, Mr Gordon Cutler, has lived here all his life, enjoying the solitude. Before his retirement he made thatching spars, an ancient craft which has largely died out. Modernization of the cottage didn't arrive until the 1990s — until then the old water pump in the kitchen was still in working order for emergency use. Mr Cutler's father was given a shilling by Thomas Hardy who showed him where he had envisaged the *Greenwood Tree*, today a magnificent beech.

Take the right fork before the cottage along a grassy track through **Yellowham Wood**. In June the way is bright with foxgloves and rhododendrons with many squirrels. Continue uphill, then, with farmland to the left and fine views ahead to the North Dorset Downs, the bridleway soon joins another wide grass track, the Ridge Way. Turn left. Soon, on the right is a new memorial seat, a good picnic place, with views east across the Piddle Valley and north to the Dorsetshire Gap and Nettlecombe Tout. Continue to a bridlepath off right which descends on a track towards a barn with wonderful horse chestnut trees on the right. At the B3142 turn right. A few yards along on the left is **Waterston Manor**.

Parts of the original Elizabethan and Jacobean building with its elaborate archways and pillars survived a fire in 1863, notably the south front with its turret-like bow over the old main entrance and parts of the east front, including the Great Gable. The house served as a rented farm for many years but is now privately owned. Its beauty and mellow appearance are due to the talent of architect Morley Horder, who blended old with new and laid out the fine gardens just before the First World War. These are occasionally open to the public.

Further on towards **Weatherbury (Puddletown)** he saw the smoke from the fire raging at **Weatherbury Farm**, the home of Bathsheba Everdene.

Hermann Lea, a photographer and personal friend of Hardy, reports a superstition of **Yellowham Wood**, which was supposed to be haunted by the 'Wild Man o' Yall'm' who fathered many of the 'love-children' born in nearby villages.

WATERSTON MANOR/WEATHERBURY FARM

Fluted pilasters, worked from the solid stone, decorated its front, and above the roof the chimneys were panelled or columnar, some coped gables with finials and like features still retaining traces of their Gothic extraction. Soft brown mosses, like faded velveteen, formed cushions upon the stone tiling ...

From one of the mullioned windows Bathsheba's head and shoulders, robed in mystic white, appeared to enquire about Fanny Robin's disappearance, and from this same window, on the morning after the marriage, Sergeant Troy *leaned idly from the lattice* to survey his newly-acquired estate – viewed by a despairing Gabriel Oak.

SHEEP-WASHING IN THE PIDDLE VALLEY

The sheep-washing pool was a perfectly circular basin of brickwork in the meadows, full of the clearest water. To birds on the wing its glassy surface, reflecting the light sky, must have been visible for miles around as a glistening Cyclops' eye in a green face ... The meek sheep were pushed into the pool by Coggan and Matthew Moon, who stood by the lower hatch, immersed to their waists; then Gabriel, who stood on the brink, thrust them under as they swam along, with an instrument like a crutch, formed for the purpose, and also for assisting the exhausted animals when the wool became saturated and they began to sink.

When the sheep were let out of the stream Cainy Ball and Joseph were

if possible wetter than the rest; they resembled dolphins under a fountain, every protuberance and angle of their clothes dribbling forth a small rill.

DRUCE FARM/LITTLE WEATHERBURY FARM

The home of Farmer Boldwood in *Far From The Madding Crowd* where he shoots Troy at the fateful Christmas engagement party.

Continue to the right along the lane through **Lower Waterston** taking care if there is traffic. Past the cottages on the left, in the second meadow, is where Hardy envisaged the sheep-washing scene in *Far From The Madding Crowd*. Here the **River Piddle** is a mere stream and unfortunately the sheep pool no longer exists although it was used until the 1970s.

Further along after a sharp left hand bend **Druce Farm** stands on the point of a bend to the right. The mellow creeper clad farmhouse stands in a beautiful walled garden.

Return across the river to the sharp bend where take the first bridleway to the left to the A35. Cross on the footbridge to follow the track or a footpath to the left into **Puddletown**.

The A35 now bypasses the village which has greatly changed from the small, thriving market town of the mid-nineteenth century: the size of its population remains roughly the same (around 1,300) but today nearly a third of these are retired. When Hardy walked here over the heath from Higher Bockhampton to visit his many relatives there were twenty bootmakers (including Hardy's uncle, John Antell), a similar number of carpenters and wheelwrights, twelve blacksmiths, several pairs of sawyers, two barrel makers and some cabinet makers. There was also a courthouse and a working mill. Today agriculture is its mainstay but the village also serves as a dormitory for Dorchester and a pleasant retirement haven with extensive building development. Only a few of the original cob and thatched cottages remain, most having been rebuilt in stone in the 1860s.

The beautiful medieval church stands near the square. It has a panelled nave roof and still boasts high box-pews, a relic of the segregation of the social classes. In the Jacobean oak musicians' gallery the old 'quire' sang and played where the present choir still sing. Hardy's grandfather — also Thomas — played the bass-viol. The quire also played at other village occasions such as weddings and barn dances.

Hardy loved the church, visiting it throughout his life, the last time being with the composer Gustav Holst in 1927. In 2004 there was a court battle backed by many villagers to block the building of a new church hall in the churchyard over several graves including that of Hardy's aunt, Maria Sparks. Ten tombstones had to be re-sited.

PUDDLETOWN/WEATHERBURY

Described by Hardy in *Far From The Madding Crowd* as it was in the 1840-50s.

By the graveyard wall of the church where several ancient yews grew Gabriel Oak met Fanny Robin as she left **Weatherbury** to follow Troy.

The north porch of the church sheltered Troy from the rain after he had planted the flowers and bulbs on Fanny's grave only to find them washed clean out of the ground the next morning by the torrent from the gargoyle's jaws – the gurgoyle –

> *too human to be called like a dragon, too impish to be like a man, too animal to be like a fiend, and not enough like a bird to be called a griffin … with a wrinkled hide … short, erect ears, eyes starting from their sockets, and its fingers and hands were seizing the corners of its mouth … to give free passage to the water it vomited.*

Today one gargoyle swallows a piece of piping to prevent regurgitation. The old tower door by which Troy told Bathsheba he attended church may well have been that visible on the west side of the tower.

Inside the church, in a box-pew near the steps to the gallery (third back, middle block), can be seen the name H-E-N-E-R-Y, carved in wood, from which Hardy created his rustic Henery Fray, who obstinately refused to spell his name in the more orthodox way.

In the poem *The Country Wedding (A Fiddler's Story)* Hardy paints a vivid picture of the church choir's participation in village events:

> *Little fogs were gathered in every hollow,*
> *But the purple hillocks enjoyed fine weather*
> *As we marched with our fiddles over the heather*
> *– How it comes back! – to their wedding that day.*

> *Our getting there brought our neighbours and all,O!*
> *Till, two and two, the couples stood ready*
> *And her father said: 'Souls, for God's sake, be steady!'*
> *And we strung up our fiddles, and sounded out 'A'.*

> *The groomsman he stared, and said, 'You must follow!'*
> *But we'd gone to the fiddle in front of the party*
> *(Our feelings as friends being true and hearty)*
> *And fiddle in front we did – all the way.*

About half a mile from Puddletown on the road eastwards towards Tolpuddle is **Athelhampton House**, one of England's finest manors dating from the fifteenth century.

It is open to the public from 10.30a.m. to 5.00 p.m. Sunday to Thursday from March 1st to the end of October (Sundays in the winter). Also on Good Friday.

The garden was designed by Inigo Jones in the seventeenth century. Hardy and his first wife, Emma, often visited the Wood-Horners who lived here from 1848-91, and whose daughter, Christine, wrote a biography *Thomas Hardy and his Two Wives*. On 4 August 1914 Hardy was dining here with his second wife, Florence, when war was declared and they noted that all present panicked because no-one had laid in provisions! **Athelhampton** is worth a short detour.

Leave **Puddletown** towards Tolpuddle then soon turn right on a minor road signposted Tincleton for about half a mile where turn left through farm gate onto a footpath uphill on right diagonal. Just before a gate the path crosses the now indistinguishable course of the old Roman road that connected Dorchester with Salisbury and London. Through the gate follow track towards **Admiston Farm**. In the farmyard take a concrete track to right. Ignore the first footpath sign on gateway on left to continue on track for a few yards where turn sharp left onto another track that leads to a thatched cottage. Pass through another gate into field in front of cottage. Follow path along side of wood with many holly and oak trees, bluebells in Spring, and views across the **Frome Valley**.

At end of wood go straight on across the undulating field with fine views back to **Puddletown Forest**. In the middle of the field is a lonely memorial stone to a soldier of the Rifle Brigade, Adrian van der Weyer, killed at Calais in 1940. Make for the northern point of a wood where pass through two gates onto a wide track between beeches. Follow this well defined track through wood and heathland for about two miles. For much of the way there is a bank on the right, some splendid beech trees and many conical pits (p. 24). The pines of **Pallington Clump** can be seen to the right just past a particularly fine spreading beech. In the eighteenth century the south-east Dorset heathland extended to over 100,000 acres; this had

Yes, from their doors by Mill-tail-Shallow,
And up Styles-Lane, and by Front-Street houses,
Where stood maids, bachelors, and spouses,
Who cheered the songs that we knew how to play.

These lanes can still be seen in **Puddletown** today. In the **Athelhampton** chantry off the south aisle of the church are the recumbent effigies of the Martyn family; Sir William, nose-less, is the old stone man beneath the toes of the children in the poem *The Children and Sir Nameless*.

ATHELHAMPTON/ATHELHALL

Athelhall is mentioned in two poems and provided features for Endelstow House in *A Pair of Blue Eyes*. It is also described in a short story *The Waiting Supper* where the *fine open-timbered roof is in a brown thicket of oak overhead*. Bellston takes Christine up a spiral stair in the thickness of the wall to view the entertainment below. The staircase existed but did not lead to the gallery.

THE FROME VALLEY/THE VALLEY OF THE GREAT DAIRIES

This stretch of the **Frome** is the Valley of the Great Dairies in *Tess of the d'Urbervilles*. Tess first approached it from the **Blackmore Vale** country further north-east:

> *The world was drawn to a larger pattern here. The enclosures numbered fifty acres instead of ten, the farmsteads were more extended, the groups of cattle formed tribes hereabout; there only families. These myriads of cows stretching under her eye from the far east to the far west outnumbered any she had ever seen at one glance before.*

Today it is still dairy country but Friesian cattle have replaced the red and dun Red Devon and Dairy Shorthorn breeds of the nineteenth century.

Hardy describes the valley in his most evocative prose:

> *the fat alluvial soil ... the languid perfume of the summer fruits, the mists, the hay, the flowers ... a vast pool of odour which at this hour seemed to make the animals, the very bees and butterflies drowsy.*

dwindled to 55,000 acres in Hardy's time. Now only 15,000 acres of true heathland remain, the rest having been swallowed by farming, forestry, army territory and urban sprawl in the coastal hinterland.

Cross straight over the B3390 to follow a minor road for about a quarter of a mile where take a bridleway to left for another quarter mile then take a very sharp right hand path (Jubilee Trail) back to road. **Culpeppers Dish**, a huge conical pit, is on the left of path before the road. Formed by the subsidence of the underlying chalk substrata by water, it is so deep that a conifer tree in the middle is below the level of the surrounding heath. Cross road to go through gate onto very steep path down through pines. Cross track towards National Grid pylons. At the next track, **Rimsmoor Pond**, which is often dry in summer, can be seen in a hollow ahead. To see **Okers Pool** continue down track where it is off to the right — very hard to find — OS Map ref. SY 813918. To continue return to Rimsmoor which keep on right to fork right straight on to a bridlegate and grassy path through the grounds of **Brickyard Cottage** (renamed **Culpepper's Cottage**). Cross the lane to a path almost directly opposite which leads to another minor road. Cross this to follow wide path through woods then over a stile into field. Follow down to another small wood. The path crosses two small streams and emerges to join downhill track to the lane between **Briantspuddle** and **Throop**. Turn right towards the hamlet of Throop. In about one-quarter of a mile, on a sharp right hand bend, go straight ahead then fork left on a track to fords. Cross these to **Turners Puddle** — one of the many villages on the **River Piddle** (or **Trent**) that bear its name. Turn right then past farm buildings left behind the farm to take first bridleway off right to **Black Hill**. Climb quite steeply up to heathland, very beautiful with heather in summer. Ignore various crosstracks to descend to a clearing in the wood. Continue down to main entrance of wood to follow the bridlepath down to **Bere Regis** cemetery. Bear right to join the **Wool-Bere road** where turn left into the town which offers pubs and accommodation.

Bere was a royal manor of the Saxon kings thus earning the suffix 'Regis'. The Domesday Book includes the manor in the royal estates inherited by William of Normandy. King John had a hunting lodge here on the field still known as **Court Green**. The Turberville family were granted the manor of Bere Regis by Henry VIII. In 1788 most of the village and all the church records were destroyed by fire, leaving few houses of earlier date. Bere

Thomas Hardy's cottage birthplace at Higher Bockhampton where the Hardy Way begins. The 1811 Ordnance Survey shows the hamlet as New Bockhampton. Drawing: Leonard Patten

Waterston Manor near Puddletown as it was before a severe fire in 1863. Both the interior and the exterior have been sensitively restored. Engraving: J.H. LeKeux, 1863

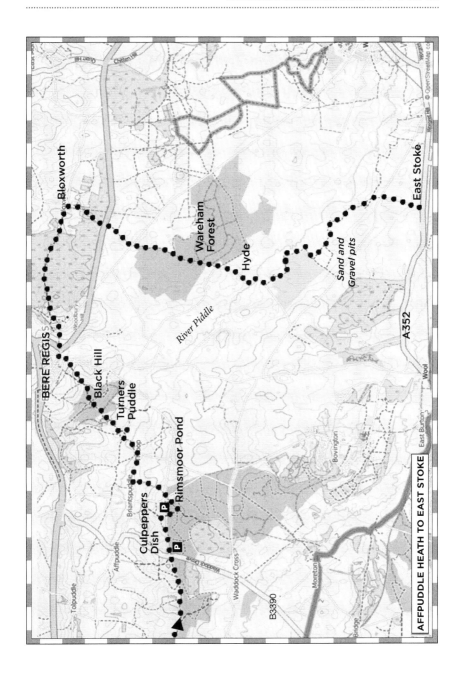

AFFPUDDLE HEATH TO EAST STOKE

PALLINGTON/CLYFFE HILL CLUMP

These pines still stand out as a landmark; they are mentioned in two poems, *Yell'ham Woods Story* and *The Paphian Ball*. Hermannn Lea saw the clump as a dividing mark between the valleys of the **Frome** and the **Pydel** in The Hardy Guides.

THE SOUTH-EAST DORSET HEATHLAND/EGDON HEATH

This is the edge of Egdon Heath country described so vividly in *The Return of the Native*, where Hardy observes it to be recorded in the Domesday Book as *heathy, furzy, briary wilderness*. There are many conical pits on the heath, some very deep, others, like these, quite shallow. Mrs Yeobright and Thomasin gather Christmas holly in a pit where *the tops of the trees were not much above the general level of the ground.*

BRICKYARD COTTAGE/ALDERWORTH

The old cottage surrounded by tall fir trees near the minor road is **Brickyard Cottage**, the **Alderworth** home of Clym and Eustacia Yeobright in *The Return of the Native*. It is built of cob and brick now covered by rendering. Nearby is a knoll with a clump of fir trees – the **Devil's Bellows** – *battered, rude, and wild* in winter but on the day when Mrs Yeobright made her ill-fated journey to **Alderworth** on a hot August afternoon *the trees kept up a perpetual moan which one could hardly believe to be caused by air.* Exhausted after her apparent rejection at the cottage she sank down wearily near **Rimsmoor Pond** then dry, where young Johnny Nunsuch brought her a drink from **Oker's Pool.** Later she struggled back towards Blooms-End, her home in the area of the Bockhamptons, only to be bitten by an adder some three miles on her way.

RIVER PIDDLE/PUDDLE/PYDEL

Hardy set his poem *A Trampwoman's Tragedy* in **Pydel Vale.**

BERE REGIS/KINGSBERE-SUB-GREENHILL

Bere Regis assumes a greater dignity when it becomes **Kingsbere-sub-Greenhill** in *Tess of the d'Urbervilles*. Greenhill is Woodbury Hill, east of the village. Jack Durbeyfield, Tess's father, learned of his illustrious d'Urberville ancestors lying in *rows and rows* in the vaults of Kingsbere-sub-Greenhill church and imagines them to be buried in *coats of mail and jewels, in gr't lead coffins weighing tons*

and Puddletown were centres of disaffection against the poor condition of the agricultural workers in the nineteenth century; there were riots and ricks were burned.

The flint and stone, mainly Perpendicular, church with its beautiful nave roof dating back to 1475 was saved from the fire. Inside the south porch hang two iron hooks from 1600 used for pulling burning thatch from cottage roofs. The church's connection with the Turberville family, who came over with the Normans, is intrinsic in *Tess of the d'Urbervilles*. On the south side in the Turberville chapel are the ancient tombs without brasses and under the large stone slab in the middle of the floor is the burial vault of the family.

Since 1893 Bere has had a thriving watercress industry.

The safest way to leave Bere to resume the route is by a safe footpath that emerges opposite the path up to **Woodbury Hill**. Opposite The Royal Oak in the High Street go down North Street then first right into Blind Street. Continue straight on to the A35. Cross carefully to climb a path straight across a field through a gate. Cross a wide track and another stile and field to the edge of a small wood. At a minor road turn right for a few yards where on the left is a stile, somewhat overgrown in summer. Cross to follow path steeply up to the edge of a wood and onto Woodbury Hill, ringed with Early Iron Age earthworks. There was a beacon here at the beginning of the nineteenth century to warn of Napoleonic invasion.

In September 1873 Hardy walked thirteen miles over the heath from Higher Bockhampton to Woodbury Hill Sheep Fair, an annual event then, dating from the Middle Ages. The fair originally took place over three weeks; in the second half of the nineteenth century it was still important for regional trading in sheep, cattle and horses as well as being a pleasure gathering; it eventually ceased to exist in the Second World War. Hardy had poignant memories of his visit as on the same evening his close friend, Horace Moule, committed suicide at Cambridge University.

Follow a left diagonal uphill to visible gateway. Through this continue on a left diagonal across field to stile, keeping farm on right. Cross stile to join track and turn left. After a few yards, opposite a bridleway sign on left, turn right down the grassy bridleway with wood on left and fine views across heathland.

and tons. His image of Kingsbere as a city loses credibility when a village youth describes it as a *little one-eyed, blinking sort o' place!*

Joan Durbeyfield, widowed, seeks lodgings here after eviction from the cottage at **Marnhull/Marlott**. The impoverished family approach from the Greenhill direction to see only *the half-dead townlet* – a view substantiated when the refugees find no accommodation and have to shelter under the south wall of the church near the huge vaults of the d'Urbervilles. The fifteenth century d'Urberville window above their heads, with its heraldic emblems, can still be seen and the altar-tomb on which Alec d'Urberville lay, pretending to be an effigy, is probably that of Robert Turberville, Lord of the Manor from 1547-59. The tombs were *canopied, altar-shaped, and plain; their carvings being defaced and broken; their brasses torn from the matrices, the rivet-holes remaining like martin-holes in a sand-cliff.* They remind Tess that her ancestors are part of the crumbling past *socially extinct.*

WOODBURY HILL/GREENHILL

Greenhill is mentioned in several Hardy novels. In *Far from the Madding Crowd* Gabriel Oak and Cainy Ball drive old Wessex horned sheep from Weatherbury (Puddletown) through the decayed old town of Kingsbere to climb the *serpentine ways* to the top of the hill. Near the ancient earthwork was a scene of great animation as shepherds from miles around gathered to trade their flocks at **Greenhill Fair** – the sheep, after their long journey,

> *bleated piteously at the unwontedness of their experiences, a tall shepherd rising here and there in the midst of them, like a gigantic idol amid a crowd of prostrate devotees.*

Elsewhere on the hill in the oval framed by the earthwork, in the midst of the hustle and bustle of the fair, was the circular tent where Sergeant Troy posed as Dick Turpin in the travelling circus and recognised his wife in the crowd as *the few yellow sunbeams … came through holes and divisions in the canvas, and spirted like jets of gold-dust across the dusky blue atmosphere of haze pervading the tent.*

Joseph Poorgrass, a simple Weatherbury labourer, was taken to the fair to cure his shyness:

> 'They took me to Greenhill Fair, and into a great gay jerry-go-nimble show, where there were women-folk riding round – standing upon horses, with hardly anything on but their smocks; but it didn't cure me a morsel.'

After about three-quarters of a mile, where track descends through rhododendron bushes, take right fork down bridleway by pine trees (ignore extreme right hand track). Here the wind soughs through the scented pines and dragonflies can sometimes be seen. In summer ragwort, heather and snapdragons abound. After about a quarter-mile go straight across a gravel track to enter further woodland between young beeches, then past larches on right to a second gravel track where again go straight on through mixed woodland, mainly oak and larches. To the left of the path, just before it emerges from the wood, is a young protected oak tree planted to replace one believed to date from Doomsday (1087).

Leave the wood through a bridlegate to cross field into **Bloxworth village**. Join the village street to pass **St Andrew's Church** surrounded by yews. This dates from the twelfth century with the tower rebuilt in the fourteenth. On the second Sunday before Christmas a carol service is held including special Dorset carols that used to be sung here and in other villages up and down the Piddle Valley in the nineteenth century. Hardy heard many tales of his own family's involvement in such activities when his grandfather was responsible for Stinsford Church's music and his father played in the 'Quire'. Christmas Eve carolling round the village often continued all night with a supper at the Hardy's cottage midway so that next morning in church the singers felt *no more than malkins* (damp rags for swabbing out an oven). This is described in *The Life of Thomas Hardy*, ostensibly written by his second wife, Florence, but which is mainly in Hardy's own words.

Continue past the old post office on the right and the old school on the left (now Bloxworth Social Club). Join another minor road but immediately go first right and follow road to the A35, about three-quarters of a mile. Cross road onto bridleway which leads through sandy heathland and afforestation. At junction with second forest track turn right and follow to road, cross and go straight on.

The next mile or so is through **Wareham Forest** with a large, often dry, marsh to the left of the track for much of the way. Continue on main track then straight on to a short footpath and then minor road for nearly a mile past the hamlet of **Hyde** to the left across the **River Piddle**. Soon take a major bridleway to the left past houses to join a track which skirts the East Dorset Golf Club. Keep left through woods and then past small lakes

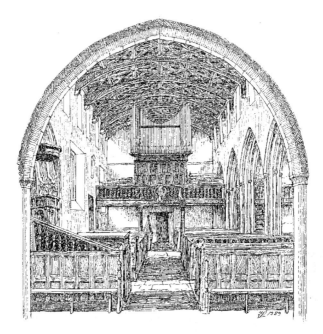

An interior view of St Mary's Church, Puddletown showing the musicians' oak gallery and the high box-pews beneath the finely timbered roof. Drawing: Fred Pitfield, 1989

Woodbury Fair as it was in the early years of the twentieth century. By 1914 the fair was no longer important for the sale of sheep, cattle and horses. Source: Rodney Legg collection

on left. At a T junction turn left (signposted to Budden's Scout Centre) to follow the bridleway which skirts a quicksand area to the right eventually reaching a large sand and gravel pit. This whole area contains many of these and the roads are busy with huge lorries. Keep clear of the pit on the right and follow on to common land where turn right up a hill to soon reach a main road. Cross with care onto a minor lane and follow for over half a mile to the A352. Turn right and cross onto pavement for another half mile where turn left down Church Lane. The former Church of St Mary the Virgin, **East Stoke**, built in 1828, has been a private residence since 1992. Further down lane cross railway at level crossing, then over the River Frome, pass the Freshwater Biological Association's River Laboratory where there is a fluvarium for the study of fish and other river life through a glass floor. Take a footpath to the right over stiles and a couple of small fields. In the next large field you can visit the remains of St Mary's Church, dating from 15thC but demolished in 1828, because it was too small for purpose, needed repairs and was subject to flooding.

Cross the field to the left hand point of a wood – the East Stoke Fen Nature Reserve – great at bluebell time and a good habitat for reed warblers. Cross brook and bear right along field side of wood then through gate and straight on to cross brook then left diagonal to far corner of field and lane. Turn right. Continue for ½ mile to the ruins of **Bindon Abbey** on right.

The 18th century Gothic House is currently leased and beautifully converted as a Health and Beauty Retreat but Hardy followers are welcome to roam the grounds of the former Abbey if they ask permission.

Weekdays and Saturdays. Tel. 01929 288629.

The remains of the twelfth century Cistercian abbey are described by Hermann Lea as they were in the early part of the twentieth century:

'The old fishponds, arched in by avenues of deciduous trees; the level grassed walks, once trodden by hordes of monks; the calm stillness which pervades the whole place; the half-obliterated foundations, marking the once extensive walls which enclosed cloister, guest-house, refectory, kitchen, hospitium, sacristy and dormitories, together with the many other offices pertaining to the Abbey — all tend to lead the mind into speculative channels of thought on the conditions of life

THE STINSFORD/MELLSTOCK CHOIR

Hardy wrote of church carol-singing in *Under The Greenwood Tree* when the choir sing round the parish of Mellstock:

> *Old William Dewy, with the violoncello, played the bass; his grandson Dick the treble violin; and Reuben and Michael Mail the tenor and second violins respectively. The singers consisted of four men and seven boys, upon whom devolved the task of carrying and attending to the lanterns, and holding the books open for the players. Directly music was the theme Old William ever and instinctively came to the front.*

> *'Now mind, neigbours,' he said, as they all went out one by one at the door, he himself holding it ajar and regarding them with a critical face as they passed, like a shepherd counting out his sheep. 'You two counter-boys, keep your ears open to Michael's fingering, and don't ye go straying into the treble part along o' Dick and his set, as ye did last year; and mind this especially when we be in "Arise and Hail" Billy Chimlen, don't you sing quite so raving mad as you fain would; and, all o' ye, whatever ye do, keep from making a great scuffle on the ground when we go into people's gates; but go quietly so as to strike up all of a sudden, like spirits ...'*

> *Then passed forth into the quiet night an ancient and time-worn hymn, embodying a quaint Christianity in words orally transmitted from father to son through several generations down to the present characters ...*

WOOLBRIDGE FARM/WELLBRIDGE MANOR

This is probably the best known of all Hardy locations. Angel Clare brought Tess here for their honeymoon and she, with a premonition of disaster, was immediately oppressed by *the mouldy old habitation* isolated in the water meadows with its mural portraits of her ancestors, the d'Urberville ladies with

> *the long pointed features, narrow eye, and smirk of the one, so suggestive of merciless treachery; the bill-hook nose, large teeth, and bold eye of the other, suggesting arrogance to the point of ferocity ...*

In reality portraits of the Turberville family still exist in the farmhouse but are in poor condition.

Angel and Tess crossed the *five yawning arches* of the bridge on their night walk and later, when Angel sleep-walks to **Bindon Abbey** (the Cistercian abbey) with

when the Abbey was in its prime, and the changes wrought by time which it must have witnessed.'

Opposite the Abbey take a well defined footpath over fields to old **Wool**. If in doubt head for a point just to the left of Wool Church. This is the point of departure from Wool on the next section of the walk. Turn right down Church Lane, then right again into Spring Street and thence to **Wool**, named from 'welle' because of the many springs in the area.

To view seventeenth century **Woolbridge Farm** leave the Station towards Wareham on the pavement of the A352. On the left is the Elizabethan bridge over the Frome. Privately owned Woolbridge Farm is just over the bridge on the left. In 1924 this was the scene of rehearsals for the first dramatisation of *Tess of the D'Urbervilles* and it is one of the most photographed of all the Hardy locations.

Woolbridge Manor House Farm, Wool adjoins a fine old 16th century bridge with five arches over the River Frome. Once the Manor was part of the monastery of Bindon Abbey and the monks exacted tolls for use of the bridge. Drawing by Douglas Snowdon.

Tess in his arms, he follows the swollen **Frome** to a footbridge where the *swift stream raced and gyrated under them, tossing, distorting, and splitting the moon's reflected face.*

Hermann Lea writes of the legend of the d'Urberville coach which is referred to by both Angel Clare and Alec d'Urberville. Tess recognises the wedding carriage as one she has seen in a dream. Angel tells her:

> *A certain d'Urberville of the sixteenth or seventeenth century committed a dreadful crime in his family coach; and since that time members of the family see or hear the old coach whenever …*

He breaks off to spare her anxiety. Alec, later, has no such scruples:

> *this sound of a non-existent coach can only be heard by one of the d'Urberville blood, and it is held to be of ill-omen to the one who hears it.*

It is easy to imagine the ghostly coach sweeping across the stone bridge to pull up outside the manor.

Portraits of Julia (left) and Frances Turberville on the walls of the staircase at Woolbridge Farm. They became the intimidating d'Urberville ancestors in Tess. Source: Dorset Year Book, 1953-54

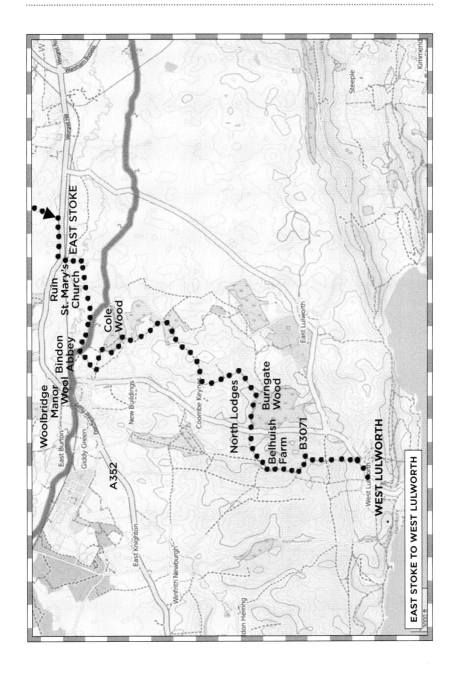

EAST STOKE TO WEST LULWORTH

BINDON ABBEY AND MILL

Angel Clare preferred to study methods at the Mill rather than be in Tess's company after her confession.

Hardy imagines Woolbridge and Bindon to be closer together when Angel bears Tess across the footbridge opposite the mill to the Abbey where he lays her in the empty stone coffin of an abbot against the north wall. This can still be seen and was the tomb of Abbot Richard Maners c.1360. Even at the time of *Tess* the ruins and surrounding area were neglected and overgrown; as Hardy observed: *The mill still worked on, food being a perennial necessity; the abbey had perished, creeds being transient.*

Hardy walked and cycled extensively in Wessex. Many of his poems were inspired by the countryside and reflect the fact that although he lived in London for quite long periods and visited regularly until just before his eightieth birthday, he was, at heart, a countryman who needed to breathe pure country air. Both his health and the flow of his writing suffered if he was away from Dorset for too long.

WEATHERS

I
This is the weather the cuckoo likes,
    And so do I;
When showers betumble the chestnut spikes,
    And nestlings fly:
And the little brown nightingale bills his best,
And they sit outside at 'The Travellers' Rest',
And maids come forth sprig-muslin drest,
And citizens dream of the south and west,
    And so do I.

II
This is the weather the shepherd shuns,
    And so do I;
When beeches drip in browns and duns,
    And thresh, and ply;
And hill-hid tides throb, throe on throe,
And meadow rivulets overflow,
And drops on gate-bars hang in a row,
And rooks in families homeward go,
    And so do I.

FROM WOOL TO WAREHAM

Leave **Wool** by the B3071 to return to the area near the church where three footpaths converge. Take the middle path signposted to Cole Wood. The path joins with another to enter the wood at its north west tip. Follow the main clearly defined path with edge of wood on right. At a cross tracks turn right but then almost immediately left at a footpath sign down past a holly tree with a fence to the left until a lane is reached at **Woodstreet Farm**. Turn right then after a few yards go through a gate on the left into a field and cross it to another gate which leads onto a sandy bridleway.

Turn right and follow uphill for nearly half a mile with views across rolling fields and small woods. As the path nears a wood it becomes very muddy at times. Enter the wood and continue straight ahead until a convergence of bridleways. Ignore the surfaced track ahead to turn sharp right to follow the bridleway up to a gate at the edge of the wood. Continue straight across a rolling field towards the only visible buildings at **Coombe Keynes**. An unsurfaced lane straight ahead over the hill serves as a guide — make for this. At a lane turn right for about one-fifth of a mile to a track (a permissive path) off to the left which is the Purbeck Way. Follow this for about a mile and a quarter to North Lodge, a ruined former gatehouse to Lulworth Castle completed in 1785. Here, turn right to follow track over two fields to reach another lodge on the edge of **Burngate Wood**. Turn right for just over a half-mile to the West Lulworth road.

Cross the road onto a lane towards **Belhuish Farm**. Pass with house on left and make for a barn where the track ends. Bear left up a field to a gate to the left of Belhuish Coppice. Through the gate follow the edge of the wood, then a hedge to a stile in the right-hand corner of the field. Over the stile turn left to take a path through a small bluebell wood. At the end of the wood go straight ahead until a gate where turn right along a grass track to a T junction with another track. There are extensive views across fine rolling downland to the coast near **Lulworth Cove**.

Continue straight ahead down the hill to **West Lulworth**, a pretty village with a Youth Hostel and plenty of other accommodation which needs to

LULWORTH COVE/LULSTEAD (LULWIND) COVE

In *Desperate Remedies* Cytherea and Owen Graye visit **Lulwind Cove** on a paddle steamer trip from Budmouth (Weymouth). The passengers disembark; Cytherea views the scene from a hill while she waits for Owen to return from **Corvsgate Castle (Corfe):**

> *Placidly spread out before her on the south was the open Channel ... dotted in the foreground by half-a-dozen small craft of contrasting rig, their sails graduating in hue from extreme whiteness to reddish brown ...*
> *Presently the distant bell from the boat was heard, warning the passengers to embark. This was followed by a lively air from the harps and violins on board, their tones, as they arose, becoming intermingled with, though not marred by, the brush of waves when their crests rolled over ...*

Hardy and his sister Mary visited **Lulworth** in the same way in 1868; similar excursions continued until 1955.

Lulwind Cove is the scene of Sergeant Troy's disappearance in *Far From The Madding Crowd*. He swims out *between the two projecting spurs of rock which formed the pillars of Hercules to this miniature Mediterranean.* He is swept out to sea where he is picked up by a brig.

The cove also features in two of the *Wessex Tales*. In *A Tradition of Eighteen Hundred and Four* the shepherd Solomon Selby lives on the downs above the bay and, as a boy, saw *Bonaparty the Corsican ogre* on the beach surveying the coastline on a secret visit.

In *The Distracted Preacher* Lulwind is a landing point for contraband where Lizzy Newberry and the reluctant young Methodist minister, Stockdale help the smugglers land tubs of brandy. Smuggling was very important to the economy of rural Dorset in the first half of the nineteenth century, approved by most, including the gentry. Its suppression caused hardship to many labourers who relied on the money they could make for being 'land-carriers'. Hardy was deeply interested in the history of smuggling, as can be seen in the poem *Winter Night in Woodland (Old Time)* where he writes of it in the context of other country pursuits such as poaching and carol-singing round the parish.

> *Out there, on the verge, where a path wavers through,*
> *Dark figures, filed singly, thrid quickly the view,*
> *Yet heavily laden; land-carriers are they*
> *In the hire of the smugglers from some nearest bay.*
> *Each bears his two 'tubs', slung across, one in front, one behind,*
> *To a further snug hiding, which none but themselves are to find.*

be booked in summer. Turn right through the village then opposite the second turning to the right (signposted Dorchester) take a lane uphill to the left. After a short distance take the right hand footpath along the side of **Bindon Hill** to **Lulworth Cove**, which is a paradise for geologists. The sea has penetrated through a fault in the hard limestone and scooped out bands of Wealden sands and clays to the chalk cliffs behind to make a circular bay — an outstanding example of the different rates of coastal erosion.

The walk continues over Army territory — following the **Range Walks** eastwards. These are open only at certain times: most weekends, the whole of August, and for about a fortnight at Christmas and a week of Easter and Spring bank holidays. It is therefore necessary to check carefully when planning this section of the walk. It is also important to keep to the authorised footpath and to follow the yellow marker posts for danger of unexploded shells.

To join the coastal path walk along the beach to climb one of the tracks to the top of the cliff. On the downs, slightly inland, just before entering the Army ranges, is the ruin of a thirteenth century chapel on the site of the original abbey of **Bindon** before the Cistercians moved to Wool in 1172. Part of the chapel was built with materials from the old abbey.

Go through the Range Walks gate and turn right towards the sea and some steps which lead down to the **Fossil Forest**. This can be viewed from the cliff, but to see the best examples of the tree stumps it is necessary to go to the east end of the ledges. The tufa-covered stumps of the shapes of fossilised trees are two hundred million years old. The information board gives details.

Continue east along the path for about a mile to above **Mupe Bay**, where there are caves that were used by smugglers, then climb steeply to the summit of **Cockpit Head** before the descent to sea level at **Arish Mell**, a gap in the chalk cliffs. Look inland to **Lulworth Castle**, for generations the property of the Weld family but built by Thomas Howard, third Viscount Bindon, in 1608. In 1927 Thomas and Florence Hardy drove there to lunch and a house-party with Mr and Mrs Weld, Hardy being most interested in all that he saw. Two years later the castle was opened to the public but

A Victorian print of a paddle-steamer in Lulworth Cove, showing the range of coastguard cottages. Source: Rodney Legg collection

Lulworth Castle was built in the early, seventeenth century by Thomas, third Viscount of Bindon. This 1789 print is by James Fittler. Source: Rodney Legg collection

was made roofless by a fire shortly afterwards. It is now again open to the public except on Saturdays.

Follow the path up a steep ascent to the top of **Flower's Barrow**, a cliff fort, the only Iron Age fortification in the **Isle of Purbeck**, an area of outstanding natural beauty of which this is the western edge. There are extensive views back to the Isle of Portland and forward to St. Aldhelm's Head. Continue for about a half a mile down to beautiful **Worbarrow Bay**. Beside the shore is a ruined cottage occupied until Christmas 1943 by retired fisherman Jack Miller who, in common with all the other inhabitants of the now deserted parish of **Tyneham** one and a quarter miles inland, was evacuated from his home by a War Cabinet decision to free the area for army manoeuvres. The Army has remained in the area ever since; the villagers were never to return to their homes. On the east side of the bay is the promontory of **Worbarrow Tout** — Tout being the old English word for look-out.

Take the track inland to **Tyneham**, which is well worth a visit and is unique. There are exhibitions in the church and the old school but otherwise it is a ghost village. Return to the coast past the toilets on the Range Walk to **Gad Cliff** to the south.

Continue on the Coast path eastwards above **Brandy Bay**, descending then past **Hobarrow Bay** to **Broad Bench**, which juts out from farmland before the path turns in towards **Kimmeridge Bay**. The Kimmeridge oil well is visible nearby, worked since 1959 by British Petroleum with an output of eighty barrels a day pumped by the tireless 'nodding donkey'. Follow the path right round the bay to the fishermen's huts on the east side which lies within the Dorset Wildlife Trust's **Purbeck Marine Wildlife Reserve** and **Fine Foundation Marine Centre**, where there are interactive displays and aquaria to encourage exploration of the bay, also a snorkelling trail.

The centre is open on Sunday afternoons only in the winter but from April to September Tuesdays-Sundays and Bank Holidays from 10.30 a.m. — 5.00 p.m.

Beneath the cliff near the huts is a waist-high stone alcove on which there is information about the industries of Kimmeridge which date back to the

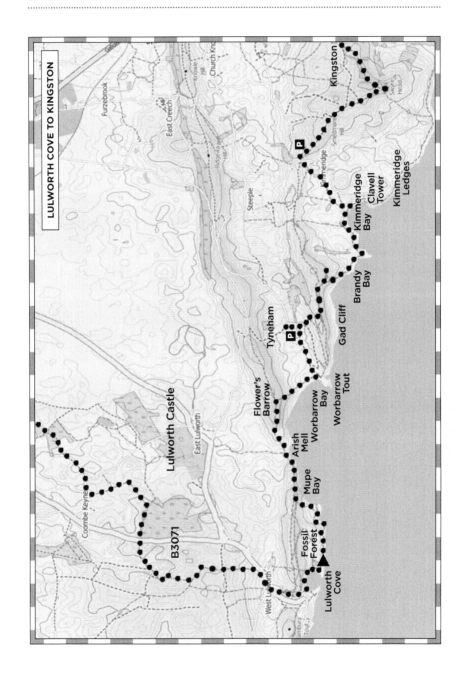

LULWORTH COVE TO KINGSTON

Iron Age. Up on the cliff is a ruined folly, the **Clavell Tower**, built in 1831 as an observatory. In 2006-2008 it was relocated 25 metres inland to save it from cliff erosion and is now available as a holiday home.

Unfortunately there has been extensive cliff subsidence along the coastal path from Kimmeridge to **Chapman's Pool** which has meant that, at the time of writing, this section of the coast path, originally also Hardy Way, is closed pending changes to make it safe again. Fortunately there is an exceptionally fine inland diversion. To avoid traffic retrace your steps back to the inland side of the cottages where take the second path to the right inland across fields keeping parallel with stream on right up to **Kimmeridge** village. Here you will find accommodation and the enterprising Clavell's Café, Restaurant and Farm Shop which is open daily throughout the year and many summer evenings. The family that run it also offer farmhouse bed and breakfast.

To get back on the path take a route between the church and the Old Parsonage on a sharp right hand bend just past the Farm Shop. In wet weather this path can be slippery. Follow up the hillside slightly to the right on a clearly defined grassy path to a T-junction where cross the lane to a minor lane straight ahead signposted Bradle Farm. After a few yards take a bridleway uphill to the right. This is the start of an amazing section of the path and I'm quite glad of the diversion. Follow the obvious route across Smedmore Hill to the **Swyre Head** Trig point, ignoring a footpath off to the left to **Kingston**. The views are stupendous: north-eastwards towards **Corfe Castle**, the **Isle of Purbeck**, right across **Poole Harbour** to **Bournemouth**: back south-westwards to the **Clavell Tower**, **Kimmeridge Ledges** and the nodding donkey. From the trig point turn left inland to follow the bridleway along the edge of **Polar Wood**. There are fine views of eighteenth century **Encombe House**, with its man-made lakes, which lies in a glorious valley between Swyre Head and **Houns-tout Cliff**. Hardy was interested in Encombe because it was owned by George Pitt, who married an heiress from Kingston Maurward in the Stinsford parish. The obelisk above the valley was erected in 1835 by Lord Eldon, then owner of the house, in memory of his brother, Sir William Scott. After the wood cross a field downhill to join a lane where there is a small car park. Turn right and follow the lane into **Kingston**.

The poem At *Lulworth Cove a Century Back* commemorates a supposed landing by the poet John Keats on his way to Rome where he died in 1821.

In the collection of stories *A Few Crusted Characters* in *The History of the Hardcomes* the drowned bodies of Stephen Hardcombe and his cousin's wife are washed ashore in the Cove. It also appears in *The Dynasts*, Hardy's epic-drama set in Napoleonic times.

THE CLAVELL TOWER

In September 1863 Hardy drew a sketch which showed a couple walking hand in hand on a path leading to the **Clavell Tower**. At this time he was more or less engaged to Eliza Nicholls, whom he had probably met in London and whose father had been a coastguard at **Kimmeridge** in the 1850s. Eliza lived in one of the coastguard cottages which can be seen slightly inland at the east end of the bay, and Hardy's early interest in smuggling may have been heightened in this period. By 1867 the romance was off, but the sketch accompanied one of his early sonnet-style poems, *She to Him 1* (1866) to the printers.

> *When you shall see me in the toils of Time,*
> *My lauded beauties carried off from me,*
> *My eyes no longer stars as in their prime,*
> *My name forgot of Maiden Fair and Free;*
>
> *When, in your being, heart concedes to mind,*
> *And judgment, though you scarce its process know,*
> *Recalls the excellencies I once enshrined,*
> *And you are irked that they have withered so:*
>
> *Remembering mine the loss is, not the blame,*
> *That Sportsman Time but rears his brood to kill.*
> *Knowing me in my soul the very same –*
> *One who would die to spare you touch of ill! –*
> *Will you not grant to old affection's claim*
> *The hand of friendship down Life's sunless hill?*

ENCOMBE HOUSE/ENCKWORTH COURT

This is the home of the elderly Lord Mountclere who marries the heroine in *The Hand of Ethelberta*. Hardy likens the exterior of the house to *a stone mask worn*

The village is dominated by its Gothic church built as a Victorian extravagance in 1880 by architect George Street, who also designed the law courts in The Strand, London. In Hardy's time a lively village with several blacksmiths, today Kingston is a very tranquil place. The old church, on a more appropriate scale for its surroundings, is at the east end of the village and is now a private dwelling. There is good food and accommodation at the Scott Arms.

Leave opposite the new church near the village pump. There are excellent views from the churchyard across to **Corfe Castle**, the Wareham Channel and Poole Harbour. **Corfe** can be seen as the guardian of the only gap in the **Purbeck Hills**, once a bastion against hostile invaders. The path to Corfe passes between a vegetable garden and a cottage; follow it down some steps then turn left past a row of attractive cottages with latticed windows. Go through a gateway then turn sharp right onto a track. Continue for a few yards then go through a kissing gate on the left down across a field keeping slightly to the right on a line to Corfe. The path to follow over **Corfe Common** can be seen as a green strip among the gorse — keep this in mind as it is the point to make for from the valley ahead. To leave the field head for the extreme right of a small stone wall at the bottom where there is a stile to cross into a small field. The path passes to the right of an animal shelter then crosses a track to another stile. Follow down the side of the hedge then over another stile into a narrow path between hedges. Veer right. This can be very muddy. Continue downhill parallel to a small stream to stiles across it into a field. Keep to the right of a hedge to pass through a gateway then straight ahead to the left hand corner of the field to a wooden and then a stone footbridge. Go slightly right in the direction of the green path seen from further back which leads up over the hill through gorse with good views of Knowle Hill to the north-west. From the top of the hill keep parallel to a lane on the left. There can be a lot of mud in the dip so keep to the left of an outcrop of gorse to join the lane in the direction of some post and rail fencing ahead. Ponies graze on the National Trust common which is a good place for a picnic. Hardy and Emma had a picnic in Corfe in 1875. Next cross a cattle grid into a lane which leads into Corfe.

Cottages of the local slate-grey limestone, some with stone roofs, cluster at the foot of the imposing ruins of the castle. It's worth spending some time

by a brick face, a brick mansion faced with Purbeck stone, a mixture of the Gothic and the Classic. His details of the interior are spurious but the cluster of buildings at **Encombe** validates Ethelberta's brother's view of the place as *a little town* with its carpenters' shops, timber-yard, and other outbuildings. Sol and his father approach **Enckworth** from the **Knollsea (Swanage)** direction after Ethelberta's wedding. From the top of a hill they look down on the *park and wood, glowing in all the matchless colours of late autumn, parapets and pediments peering out from a central position afar.* They descend to discover that:

> *Exclusiveness was no part of the owner's instincts; one could see that at a glance. No appearance of a well-rolled garden path attached to the park-drive ... The approach was like a turnpike road, full of great ruts, clumsy mendings; bordered by trampled edges and incursions upon the grass at pleasure. Butchers and bakers drove as freely herein as peers and peeresses. Christening parties, wedding companies, and funeral trains passed along by the doors of the mansion without check or question.*

Lord Mountclere, born to the place, is careless of outward appearances. *Wild untidiness* prevails.

KINGSTON/LITTLE ENCKWORTH/KINGSCREECH

In *The Hand of Ethelberta* **Kingston** is **Little Enckworth**, where Sol Chickerel brings the brougham to aid his sister Ethelberta's flight from Lord Mountclere when she discovers that he keeps a mistress in the grounds of Enckworth Court. *Ethelberta came from the little door by the bush of yew* – this was near the north lodge of Enckworth somewhere near the path which leads from Houns-tout to the village. There are many yews hereabouts; trees sacred to the Druids and used for making longbows in medieval England.

In one of Hardy's finest short stories **Old Mrs Chundle**, Kingston is **Kingscreech**. In this the old church (rebuilt in 1833 on the site of a twelfth century chapel) is where the young curate attempts to surmount Mrs Chundle's deafness by various devices, finally using a speaking tube to her ear from the pulpit. This is a disaster when he is assailed by her bad breath! The old woman is more than a match for him in this humorous story, which is deeply observant of human nature.

The dominating Victorian Church of St James in the small village of Kingston. Built in Purbeck stone and marble, it was completed in 1880. Drawing: Alfred Dawson, 1882

Encombe superbly situated in a sheltered valley east of Kimmeridge. Completed in 1770 for the Pitt family, it was sold in 1807 to John Stott, later the first Earl of Eldon. Drawing: W. Tompkins c.1800

CORFE/CORVSGATE

In *Desperate Remedies* Owen Graye misses the Lulwind steamboat because he misjudges the distance when he walks to **Corvsgate Castle** that *interesting mediaeval ruin.*

Ethelberta rides on a *rather sad-looking donkey* from Knollsea to Corvsgate to attend a meeting of the Imperial Archaeological Association to which she has been invited by Lord Mountclere. Her route along **Nine Barrow Down** can be seen from **Knowle Hill** where the path leads after Corfe. As she approaches the castle

> *The towers of the notable ruin to be visited rose out of the furthermost shoulder of the upland as she advanced, its site being the slope and crest of a smoothly nibbled mount at the toe of the ridge she had followed.*

She ties the ass to a stone projecting from the castle wall to climb to the top.

> *Once among the towers above, she became so interested in the windy corridors, mildewed dungeons, and the tribe of daws peering invidiously upon her from overhead, that she forgot the flight of time.*

The aristocratic party that assembles beneath find her donkey which has broken loose. Embarrassed she disclaims all knowledge of it, an act of betrayal for which she feels inwardly ashamed. Later when the others have gone Ethelberta remains to sketch the landscape between the ragged walls.

The **Castle Inn** at Corvsgate, now on the main road to Swanage, is where Ethelberta's sister, Picotee, waits for her brother Sol who is summoned to Enckworth to aid Ethelberta's escape.

here; there is plenty of accommodation but it needs to be booked in the summer season. This is Enid Blyton country and there is currently A Ginger Pop Shop.

The site of the castle as a fortification dates back to Saxon times. In 978 seventeen-year-old King Edward was knifed in the back here in a family plot to seize the throne for his brother Ethelred (the Unready). The corpse of the young king was taken to Wareham, then Shaftesbury, where it became renowned as a source for miracles. Edward was made a saint and martyr although he had done nothing to deserve such honours. In the market place the village sign commemorates St Edward. Part of the castle dates from the time of William the Conqueror; the rest was added later. It was a Royal Castle often used as a hunting lodge and as a prison. Held by the Royalists in the Civil War, it fell to the Parliamentarians who ordered its demolition in 1646. A shell remains that has been also attacked by the elements but it is still an impressive sight. Ravens were here until the mid-nineteenth century. It was bequeathed to the National Trust in 1981 as part of the vast Corfe Castle estate which comprises fifty cottages in the town, Corfe Common, Purbeck stone quarries and nine miles of coastline as well as extensive heathland nature reserves and amenity woodland. There is a scaled reconstruction of the castle and a model village off the Market Square behind the newsagents.

Other places of interest are the church of **St Edward the Martyr**, the town hall next to it and West Street itself, which was the centre of a stone trade in the Middle Ages. Purbeck marble was worked to make effigies and monumental stonework for churches. The church is a Victorian restoration except for the fifteenth century tower and carved west doorway. Charles II's coat of arms is over the north door and there is a statue of Edward above the east gable, carved in the 1920s. The town hall, the smallest in England, was built in 1774 of stone and brick; it has a council chamber on the first floor and a small museum on the ground floor.

Until the Reform Act of 1832 Corfe was one of the infamous rotten boroughs — places which returned a disproportionate number of Members of Parliament to their population — Corfe, with 1,700 people, had two MPs whereas Sheffield, Birmingham and Manchester had none!

Corfe Common with the village and castle in the background. In medieval times marble was quarried here. Drawing: Alfred Dawson, 1882

Corfe Castle dominates this nineteenth century rural landscape. Hardy's 'Corvsgate' was the original Saxon name. Engraving: J.H. LeKeux, 1861

Leave the town by a footpath to the left from the main entrance to the castle to follow round the base of the hill to a lane. Just before a stone bridge cross a wooden bridge then bear left to join a path to the left that leads through a gate along the side of West Hill. Follow a broad track uphill to a gate into a thicket. Next fork right uphill on a byway towards **Knowle Hill**. In spring and early summer a blaze of yellow gorse lights the hillside. The next half mile is close-cropped springy turf and panoramic views, south to the sea towards Kimmeridge, south-east to Swanage along Nine Barrow Down and back to Kingston, its church an unmistakeable landmark. Down in the near valley is the village of Church Knowle. Pass a stone commemorating Mary Baxter of The Ramblers' Association.

Now the panorama opens up to the north-east to reveal the Wareham Estuary, Poole Harbour with its islands and bird sanctuaries and the Bournemouth coast. Continue straight ahead down track through gate to just before lane where go through a small metal gate on the right and follow path down the side of the hill towards East Creech.

At the Furzebrook road turn right. Further along on the right is a memorial stone with the names of GHQ Auxiliary Unit operational patrol which operated in this area of Purbeck during the Second World War. If there had been an invasion, this unit, comprised of local men who knew the Church Knowle area well, would have gone into hiding then operated behind enemy lines to attack the enemy's lines of communication and supply. The unit had a hidden underground operation base in nearby Norden Woods — the remains can still be seen.

Less than a quarter of a mile on there is an entrance into the wood on the right where a bridleway and a footpath begin. Take the path that runs parallel to the road for the next quarter-mile. This can get very muddy but is interesting as it is on the property of the British Herpetological Society, the **Green Pool**, an ideal habitat for the study of reptiles and amphibians. Pools are on both sides of the path.

Continue along the road. A lane to the right leads to the **Blue Pool**, a lake formed by old clay workings. Its vivid turquoise and blue colour is caused by diffracted light passing through minute particles of clay suspended in the water.

It's open from March to November with a café.

In *Far From The Madding Crowd* there are many vivid descriptions of sheep-rearing. Hardy knew a great deal about this subject and was sensitive to the many difficulties that shepherds encountered. He wrote this poem a few weeks before his death.

AN UNKINDLY MAY

A shepherd stands by a gate in a white smock-frock:
He holds the gate ajar, intently counting his flock.

The sour spring wind is blurting boisterous-wise,
And bears on it dirty clouds across the skies;
Plantation timbers creak like rusty cranes,
And pigeons and rooks, dishevelled by late rains,
Are like gaunt vultures, sodden and unkempt.
And song-birds do not end what they attempt:
The buds have tried to open, but quite failing
Have pinched themselves together in their quailing.
The sun frowns whitely in eye-trying flaps
Through passing cloud-holes, mimicking audible taps.
'Nature, you're not commendable today!'
I think. 'Better tomorrow!' she seems to say.

That shepherd still stands in white smock-frock,
Unnoting all things save the counting his flock.

GREEN POOL

When Hardy was young there were many more snakes and newts in the heathland around the cottage at Higher Bockhampton. One hot day a snake was found curled up on baby Thomas in his cradle, both asleep. When walking through Green Pool remember this short, simple poem from Uncollected Poems.

THE LIZARD

If on any warm day when you ramble around
Among moss and dead leaves, you should happen to see
A quick trembling thing dart and hide on the ground,
And you search in the leaves, you would uncover me.

Straight on just past a works entrance on the right and a house take a footpath to the left to follow the Purbeck Way across Creech Heath. After passing some houses cross the railway line and bear right over Stoborough Heath. Cross the A351 then fork right keeping on the Purbeck Way to cross the B3075 onto a minor lane. Follow straight on the Purbeck Way to Wareham turning left into Ridge — about two miles to the east is Slepe Heath, typical Hardy heathland recently acquired by the National Trust. Turn left to follow the south bank of the River Frome into **Wareham**.

There has been a settlement on this low ridge between the **Rivers Piddle** and **Frome** since the Iron Age. The town has earthen defences on three sides, built by the Saxons after Viking pirates had captured the port in 876. Wareham was then an important place and its massive walls are the best preserved of all the defences in King Alfred's Burghal Hidage. Later these were stone capped but were reduced by the Parliamentarians in the Civil War in the seventeenth century. The town claims to have been besieged more than any other in England. In 1685, after the Monmouth rebellion against James II, five rebels were executed by order of Judge Jeffreys at Bloody Bank on the **West Walls**. The grassy mounds are now an interesting walk.

Wareham was a port until the fourteenth century, after which, because of larger ships and river silting, it was gradually superseded by Poole. A bad fire in 1762 destroyed much of the town; only two thatched cottages remain. Many of the houses date from the late eighteenth and early nineteenth centuries. Worth looking for are the almshouses on East Street (1741), the Black Bear Hotel with its huge bear (1770) and an early Georgian three storey manor house in South Street opposite the 1830 Unitarian Chapel which is now the Conservative Club. **St Martin's Church** in North Street is the most complete example of a Saxon church in Dorset. The chancel and nave date from 1030; the wall paintings from the 12th century. The fine life-sized effigy of T.E.Lawrence (Lawrence of Arabia) in Arab dress by his friend the artist, official war artist and sculptor Eric Kennington, is enhanced by the simple tranquillity of the place.

WAREHAM/ANGLEBURY

In *Desperate Remedies* Owen Graye walks on to **Anglebury** from Corvsgate Castle to try to catch a late train back to Budmouth. Failing this he later attempts a walk back along the railway line. Long walks were commonplace in the nineteenth century. The steward, Manston, meets a postman near Anglebury station who, over the age of forty-five, walks twenty-two miles a day to deliver the post:

> 'Yes – a long walk – for though the distance is only sixteen miles on the straight – that is, eight to the furthest place and eight back, what with the ins and outs to the gentlemen's houses, it makes two-and-twenty for my legs. Two-and twenty miles a day, how many a year? I used to reckon it, but I never do now. I don't care to think o' my wear and tear, now it do begin to tell upon me.'

The **Red Lion** at Anglebury is still there today at the central crossroads, as located in The Hand of Ethelberta:

> The 'Red Lion' as the inn or hotel was called which of late years had become the fashion among tourists, because of the absence from its precincts of all that was fashionable and new, stood near the middle of the town, and formed a corner where in winter the winds whistled and assembled their forces previous to plunging helter-skelter along the streets. In summer it was a fresh and pleasant spot, convenient for such quiet characters as sojourned there to study the geology and beautiful natural features of the country round.

An hostler and a milkman see Ethelberta set out for a walk along the highway across the **Froom** water-meadows with her *clane-washed face … and … her hair up in a buckle.*

Something of the lively atmosphere of the old coaching inns can be gleaned from the conversation between the hostler, John, *a little bow-legged old man*, and the simple stable-boy, David Straw, as they dispatch first Lord Mountclere and Sol Chickerel and then Christopher Julian and Ethelberta's father towards Knollsea.

> 'What slap-dash jinks may there be going on at Knollsea, then, my sonny?' said the hostler to the lad, as the dog cart and the backs of the two men diminished on the road. 'You be a Knollsea boy: have anything reached your young ears about what's in the wind there, David Straw? … do you know why three folk, a rich man, a middling man, and a poor man, should want horses for Knollsea afore seven o'clock in the morning on a blinking day in Fall, when everything is

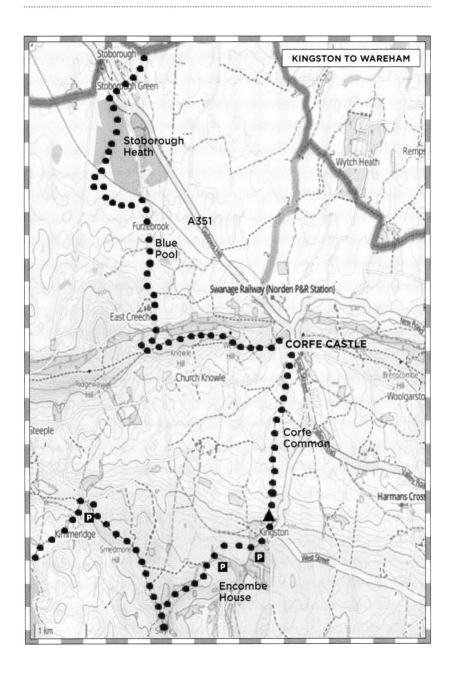

as wet as a dishclout, whereas that's more than often happens in fine summer weather?'

'No, – I don't know, hostler.'

'Then go home and tell your mother that ye be no wide-awake boy and that old John, who went to school with her father afore she was born or thought o' says so … Chok' it all, why should I think there's sommat going on at Knollsea ? Honest travelling have been so rascally abused since I was a boy in pinners, by tribes of nobodies tearing from one end of the country to Pother, to see the sun go down in salt water, or the moon play jack-lantern behind some rotten tower or other, that upon my song, when life and death's in the wind there's no telling the difference!'

St Martin's Church, Wareham, believed to have been founded by St Aldhelm in 698. Photograph: Walter Pouncy, in the 1890s

FROM WAREHAM TO WIMBORNE

Leave Wareham from the railway station. Cross the track at the pedestrian crossing to a mini roundabout. Alongside the road to the Westminster Road Industrial estate take the concrete cycleway near conifer trees. At a fork bear left then cross a road to Tantinoby Lane which becomes a path. After a children's play area leave the main path to cross an open space on a visible path under the national grid to the left of a pylon to join a road, then straight across at a T-junction. Follow the track uphill to **Northport Heath** which is part of **Wareham Forest** owned by the Drax Estate and loaned to the Forestry Commission. The area is criss-crossed with paths and cycle tracks used by many walkers and cyclists but there are no rights of way in this area and there are no Hardy Way signs. At most times it's possible to cross northwards to the bridleway which runs westwards from Sherford Bridge on the B3075 but take care when forestry work is taking place. Firstly then turn right keeping the golf course on right. At the bottom of a hill bear left to continue for just over half a mile along the edge of the forest to a T junction after a bridge. The track veers slightly to the left then straight ahead for about one-and-a-half miles. This passes along the western edge of **Morden Bog** near a conifer plantation named **Parsons Pleasure** after Frank Parsons, Chief Forester of Wareham from 1950-1968, who proved that this water-logged heathland could be made productive by mechanical draining and fertilising. Unfortunately the essence of the heath is lost through such afforestation, but the **Decoy Heath** on the right is still wild marshland and now a National Nature Reserve. Some way before the power lines divert a short way on a path to the right to view the **Old Decoy Pond**. Just before passing beneath the power lines take a left fork and go straight on to join a bridleway where turn left.

After about three quarters of a mile up a hill turn right on the Wareham Forest Way towards **Woolsbarrow Hill Fort**, the location of an Iron Age settlement. Continue straight ahead then bear right past a sewage works to follow the Wareham Forest way to the A35. The path turns right parallel to the road for nearly half a mile then crosses it on the clearly marked route left which leads to a lane. Turn right into **East Morden**.

DECOY HEATH, MORDEN

In *The Hand of Ethelberta* Ethelberta crossed the railway at Anglebury and soon got into a lonely heath. She becomes absorbed in watching a hawk preying on a wild duck and follows their progress to the **Decoy Heath** some three miles north-west. When the hawk strikes

Ethelberta now perceived a whitely shining oval of still water, looking amid the swarthy level of the heath like a hole through a nether sky.

The duck dives into the pool to evade the hawk. By now dusk is approaching and Ethelberta is lost. She meets Christopher Julian, her former lover, who returns her to the path for Anglebury.

Hardy knew that in a world of scientific 'progress', hemmed in by increasing urbanisation, man desperately needs wild places to which he can retreat from time to time to feel the strength and beauty of the natural world.

To recline on a stump of thorn in the central valley of Egdon, between afternoon and night, as now, where the eye could reach nothing of the world outside the summits and shoulders of heathland which filled the whole circumference of its glance, and to know that everything around and underneath had been from prehistoric times as unaltered as the stars overhead, gave ballast to the mind adrift on change, and harassed by the irrepressible New.

Few truly wild parts of the heath remain, but the Decoy Heath with its pools and bogs still retains the primitive spirit that Hardy recognised and loved.

Creech Barrow from the Wareham Road – terrain typical of Hardy's Egdon Heath. Drawing: Alfred Dawson, 1882

'The Cock and Bottle' is a short way to the right if refreshment is required. If not cross straight over lane then in a short distance turn left at Sellers Farm across stile next to gate. Follow uphill across grassy farmyard to small stile then along side of field towards cottages. Just before top of field go through small gap to stile on right to turn left along New Lane to the main part of the village. Turn right past Church Villa with its five Elizabethan chimneys, and the church, rebuilt in 1873 with a rather austere exterior but light and airy inside with a kneeling monument of a rotund Sir Thomas Erle, owner of **Charborough Park** in the late sixteenth century.

Leave Morden past a line of cottages to a T junction where turn right up a hill along a shady lane which dips and then rises to a sharp right-hand bend. Here leave the lane for a footpath straight ahead up through a wood (ignore the track). Cross a stile into the left-hand field through a bridle gate, keeping the hedge/fence to the right. Near a swampy pool on the left a copse of sweet chestnuts and oaks is bright with foxgloves in early summer. After a short section on the track, just past a bend, turn right through a gateway into a wood where immediately take a footpath to the left. Follow the edge of the wood from where **Charborough Tower** can be seen among conifers to the left. The path soon enters the wood in which there are deer and grey squirrels. Continue down over two stiles to a track where turn left keeping on the Wareham Forest Way. Proceed over more stiles and two fields to follow power lines to a lane. The medieval church of St Mary **Lytchett Matravers** is on the right: this was the site of the old village of Lytchett which was wiped out during the Black Death in the fourteenth century. Sir John Maltravers, who murdered King Edward II in 1327, is buried beneath the floor of the north aisle.

Cross the lane and go straight ahead. Here there is a choice: either to take the direct route on the lane all the way to the village of **Sturminster Marshall** or, just over half-a-mile further on, on a sharp left hand bend, branch off on the Wareham Forest Way to the village, which is more interesting but involves two short stretches on busy roads and, when I attempted to walk it in May, the route was impassable in one place over an arable field. If you decide to remain on the lane, which I recommend, about a mile along on the left is an entrance to **Charborough Park**, a private estate long owned by the Drax family. In the grounds is the Grove Ice-House where the overthrow of James II was plotted in 1686.

CHARBOROUGH TOWER/RINGS-HILL SPEER

The tower is the focal setting for the love affair of Lady Viviette Constantine and the young astronomer, Swithin St Cleeve, who uses it as an observatory in *Two on a Tower.* Hardy claimed that the tower was based on *two or three originals – Horton, Charborough, etc.* The descriptions of the tower in the novel seem nearest to **Charborough** whereas the location resembles that of **Ring's-Hill Speer** near **Millborne St Andrew** on the Blandford Forum to Dorchester road. Charborough Tower was erected in 1790 as an ornamental folly and rebuilt in 1839 after being struck by lightning. It is 120 feet high and described in the novel as *in the Tuscan order of classical architecture* although in fact only partly resembling Tuscan. Hermann Lea visited it and wrote:

'A heavy moulded handrail guides us to the top, where we enter a room panelled in chestnut and fitted with some handsomely carved seats, from whence the view is seen through many windows.'

CHARBOROUGH HOUSE/WELLAND HOUSE

Hardy gives very little description of Viviette's home, **Welland House**. In fact he was not familiar with Charborough when the novel was written, but in 1895, when making sketches for the frontispiece of the Wessex edition, he sent a Scot, Macbeth Raeburn, to sketch Charborough. The owner was jealous of access but the bailiff, from the same Scottish village as Raeburn, allowed him to sketch as long as the 'queer auld body' couldn't see! Over thirty years later Hardy and Florence dined here, one of his last engagements.

Charborough House, invisible from the route, dates from the seventeenth century. The tower can be seen on the left. Engraving: J.H. LeKeux, 1868

Continue along the lane to cross the A31(T) and then the A350 into the village of **Sturminster Marshall**. On the right is the **Bailey Gate Industrial Estate**. In the 1960s the cheese factory here was the second largest in Europe, capable of producing 20 tons of cheese per day. The railway was axed in the mid-sixties; cheese making ceased in 1975.

Further along at the corner of Churchill Close are **Johnny and Joe's Cottages**, named after an eleven year old child, John Joseph, who died of influenza in a private school at Lytchett. Near No. 110 High Street is a stone which shows the depth of floodwater from the **River Stour** on 19 January 1980 — 250 yards from the river.

The village has three pubs, a general store and two village greens. One of these can be seen where the road converges with several others. This was the site of an annual fair held the week after Whitsun from 1101 to about 1800. A maypole has stood here for centuries; the present one, with a seat at its base, was erected in 1986 to replace one renewed for Queen Victoria's Diamond Jubilee in 1897. The water rat weather vane is the emblem of the village.

Continue to the north-east past the red brick building of the **Old Charity School** endowed at the end of the eighteenth century and erected in 1832. Also on the right is an attractive curve of cottages rebuilt after a fire in 1976. Opposite, the **Church of St Mary** is a mixture of medieval (the aisle and nave walls) and nineteenth century restoration (most of the windows, the tower and the piers). The yew tree by the lychgate was planted on the day of Queen Victoria's funeral in 1901.

The lane crosses the Stour over **White Mill Bridge**, medieval, with eight arches, parapets and a transportation plaque. You are now on National Trust land and on the left is the restored **White Mill**.

It is open at weekends and on Bank Holidays from 12 noon to 5.00 p.m.

Veer left to follow the main lane north-east. Keep on the main lane with the White Mill car park on the right then take a right turning to follow lane for about half a mile where turn right opposite a minor lane to Shapwick onto a beech-lined bridleway. Continue for three-quarters of a mile then turn right at a T junction to reach a lane after another half-mile. Turn left

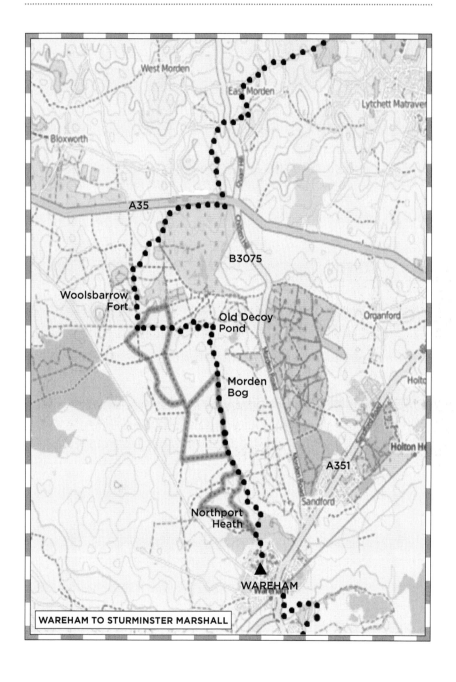

WAREHAM TO STURMINSTER MARSHALL

for about three-quarters of a mile to **St Stephen's Church**, Kingston Lacy. For the past mile or so the route has bordered the grounds of one of Dorset's most impressive houses, **Kingston Lacy**, always tantalisingly invisible. The seventeenth century house was built for the Bankes family following irreparable damage to Corfe Castle during the Civil War. The keys to the castle are still in the library, never surrendered to the Parliamentarians. The house was altered in the 1830s by Sir Charles Barry, the architect of the Houses of Parliament. Thomas and Florence Hardy visited Mrs Bankes here in the autumn of 1926. It was bequeathed to the National Trust by Ralph Bankes in 1981.

The house is open to the public most days between Wed-Sun from mid-March to early November but check dates on the website. The beautiful 250 acre park is open most of the year. The entrance is on the B3082 Wimborne-Blandford road.

There is a memorial to the Bankes family in the churchyard of St Stephen's church, which has some grotesque gargoyles on its tower. Turn right at the church along an avenue of 150-year-old oaks which line **Pamphill Green**, the estate village of Kingston Lacy, tranquil and unspoiled with seventeenth and eighteenth century thatched cottages scattered around the main village green and two commons, **Little Pamphill** and **Cowgrove**. When the lane forks go past Pamphill First School, built in 1698 when the centre part was a school with almshouses on each side. Just before a thatched cottage near the Vine Inn turn left to pass directly beneath an electricity pylon then right through a wood. At cross paths turn right at bottom of steps before the stile then down over more stiles and out of the wood into a field where turn right with a small stream on right to join a lane at the bottom of the field. Cross the lane to another stile to continue straight ahead and then left on to the **Stour Valley Way.** Follow a pretty riverside path towards **Wimborne Minister** visible ahead. To the left, above the lane just crossed, is **Farrs House** built in the eighteenth century. At productive allotments keep to the right-hand fork of the path to join a road. Turn left into **Wimborne**.

In June 1881, after three years in London, Hardy and Emma returned Dorset. The previous autumn he had been seriously ill and was only just recovering. They leased **Llanherne**, a Victorian brick villa in **The Avenue** (now **12 Avenue Road** off the B3073 to Ringwood) in the south-east of

FARRS HOUSE/YEWSHOLT LODGE

Yewsholt Lodge was where Barbara of the House of Grebe waited for her young husband to return from Italy with terrible facial injuries sustained in a fire, in one of Hardy's stories about aristocratic women, *A Group of Noble Dames*. The house was occupied by the army during the Second World War but has since been restored and is now used as business premises. It still has a *central hall with a wooden gallery running round it* and Hardy describes it as *standing on a slope so solitary, and surrounded by trees so dense, that the birds who inhabited the boughs sang at strange hours, as if they hardly could distinguish night from day.*

WIMBORNE/WARBORNE

In *Two on a Tower* **Wimborne** features as **Warborne** where Swithin St Cleeve attended the grammar school, a place, according to Haymoss, a local, *'where they draw up young gam'sters' brains like rhubarb under a ninepenny pan ... hit so much larnin into en that 'a could talk like the day of Pentecost'.* The school was founded in 1496 as part of the chantry of the Minster by Lady Margaret Beaufort, mother of Henry VII. A new charter was granted by Elizabeth I in 1562 after the suppression of the chantries under Henry VIII. The original stone building was rebuilt in 1851 in red brick and remained in use as Queen Elizabeth's Grammar School until 1977. It is now private accommodation.

The **Minster** inspired two poems. *The Levelled Churchyard* is a poetical attack on the practice of uprooting tombstones and moving them to other places to pave some path or porch or to line the base of the exterior walls of the church. The corpses complain:

> *Oh Passenger, pray list and catch*
> *Our sighs and piteous groans,*
> *Half stifled in this jumbled patch*
> *Of wrenched memorial stones!*

> *We late-lamented, resting here,*
> *Are mixed to human jam,*
> *And each to each exclaims in fear,*
> *'I know not which I am!'*

Wimborne near the Stour and convenient for the railway station and visits to London. The house stands today virtually unchanged with a plaque to commemorate the Hardys' two years occupancy. Cherry trees line the avenue having long replaced the limes that Hardy remembered. On the night of their arrival the Hardys watched Tebbutt's Comet from the garden, an event which no doubt contributed to the evolution of *Two on a Tower*, written at Llanherne, a romantic tragic-comedy that appeared in 1882 described by Hardy in the preface as *infinitesimal lives against the stupendous background of the stellar universe*.

Hardy often worked under the vine on the stable wall of the large and fruitful garden with its Canterbury Bells, Sweet Williams and profusion of summer fruits, strawberries, cherries, currants, gooseberries, even peaches.

Wimborne Minster dates from the early eighth century when a double monastery for monks and nuns was founded by Cutbergh, sister of King Ina of Wessex. **The Cornmarket** (1738), north-west of the Minster, is the site of the original market place and stocks. Today Wimborne is famous for its large, covered markets held on Friday, Saturday mornings and Sunday mornings. There are many good eighteenth and nineteenth century buildings; the best street is **West Borough**, north of the **Square**. Parts of the **Priest's House** local history museum in the High Street date from the early seventeenth century including, in the parlour, a plaster ceiling with a frieze inscription PEOPLE REFRAYN FROM SYN.

The **Minster** is mainly Norman, built in grey and rich brown stone. When house-hunting Hardy *entered it at ten at night, having seen a light within, and sat in a stall listening to the organist practising, while the rays from the musician's solitary candle streamed across the arcades*. Hardy's architectural training and his innate feeling for history and appreciation of beauty made him deeply opposed to insensitive church restoration. Many years later in 1906, in a paper for the Society for the Protection of Ancient Buildings, he wrote: *At Wimborne Minster fine Jacobean canopies were removed from Tudor stalls for the offence only of being Jacobean.*

The Minster has many outstanding features. In the north chapel is the debonair reclining figure of Sir Edmund Uvedale in armour. On the north side of the bell tower stands the wooden figure of the **Quarter Jack**,

The humour gains momentum:

The wicked people have annexed
  The verses on the good;
A roaring drunkard sports the text
  Teetotal Tommy should!

Here's not a modest maiden elf
  But dreads the final trumpet,
Lest half of her should rise herself,
  And half some sturdy strumpet!

In *Copying Architecture in an Old Minster* Hardy refers to the **Quarter Jack**:

How smartly the quarters of the hours march by
  That the jack-o'-clock never forgets;
  Ding-dong; and before I have traced a cusp's eye,
Or got the true twist of the ogee over,
  A double ding-dong ricochetts.

Just so did he clang here before I came,
  And so will he clang when I'm gone
Through the Minster's cavernous hollows – the same
Tale of hours never more will he deliver
  To the speechless midnight and dawn!

In St George's chapel Hardy saw the arms of the Fitz Piers family of Hinton Martell, a few miles north of Wimborne. He later used the name for Grace Melbury's unfaithful husband, the doctor Edred Fitzpiers, in *The Woodlanders*.

Hardy wrote nostalgically of his home in Wimborne when in 1918 he recalled the young lime trees that were planted in The Avenue during the 1880s:

They are great trees, no doubt, by now,
  That were so thin in bough –
    That row of limes –
  When we housed there; I'm loth to reckon when;
The world has turned so many times,
  So many, since then!

dressed as a grenadier of the British Army at the time of the Napoleonic wars, a hammer in each hand with which it strikes the bells every quarter hour. There is a twenty-four hour astronomical clock on the south wall of the baptistery built in 1320 by a monk in Glastonbury. Though still accurate it shows the earth at the centre of the universe. The sides are Elizabethan and it was redecorated in 1979. Above the south vestry is a rare chained library of some 250 volumes, dating from 1686.

White Mill Bridge across the River Stour at Sturminster Marshall. The mill nearby is now open to the public in the afternoon at weekends and on bank holidays. Drawing: H.S. Joyce

The nave of Wimborne Minster as it was in 1875 when Hardy listened to the
organist practising. In 1965 the pipes were modified by the addition of brass
tubes like trumpets projecting at right angles near the top. Recitals are sometimes
broadcast from the Minster. Drawing: Nathaniel Whittock

Llanherne, Avenue Road, Wimborne, the residence of Thomas and Emma Hardy from 1881–83. The plaque commemorating their years here is clearly visible. Photograph: Rodney Legg

Badbury Rings is an Iron Age hillfort dating from about 800 BC, owned by the National Trust. It was in use until the Roman occupation of AD 43.

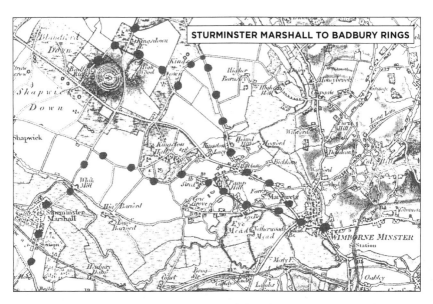

STURMINSTER MARSHALL TO BADBURY RINGS

This majestic avenue of beeches was planted near Badbury Rings in 1835. Over 720 trees were planted and stretch for two and a half miles along the Blandford to Wimborne road.

FROM WIMBORNE TO CRANBORNE

Leave Wimborne from the Square along West Street near the King's Head Hotel. Soon turn right along Victoria Road. On the left, just past Cowgrove Road, is **St Margaret's Chapel**, formerly a thirteenth century leper hospital. Continue along the B3082, over the traffic lights and past Queen Elizabeth's School. After about a quarter mile take the second small turning to the right which leads north-west, through National Trust land, to Chilbridge Farm nearly a mile ahead past several attractive thatched cottages.

Continue on a wide track straight ahead with the farm to the left. When the track meets a lane turn left for just over half a mile, with Bronze Age burial mounds in field to the right. At crosstracks turn right. After a wood on left go straight on past small cottage for a short way to soon turn left on a bridleway towards **Badbury Rings**. To visit turn right on a footpath which leads to the Rings, an Iron Age hillfort, part of the Kingston Lacy estate. From here can be seen the wonderful avenue of beeches planted by William John Bankes in 1835, which stretches for over two miles on the Wimborne-Blandford road. There was also a Roman settlement here and nearby is the junction of two Roman roads: one from Dorchester to Old Sarum, near Salisbury, and London, the other from Bath to Hamworthy (Poole).

In July 1881 Hardy, Emma and his sister, Kate, visited Badbury in a wagonette hired at the George in Wimborne, driven by a former postilion on the Blandford to Wimborne coach.

Leave Badbury on a bridleway that leads north east from the car park. Go straight on keeping left of **The Oaks**, an ancient woodland planted at the beginning of the fourteenth century, now managed by the National Trust who utilise grazing and natural regeneration to maintain an ecological balance. Soon the path joins the route of the old Roman Road from Dorchester to Old Sarum, which stretches visibly ahead for a considerable distance. Bear left towards a white house.

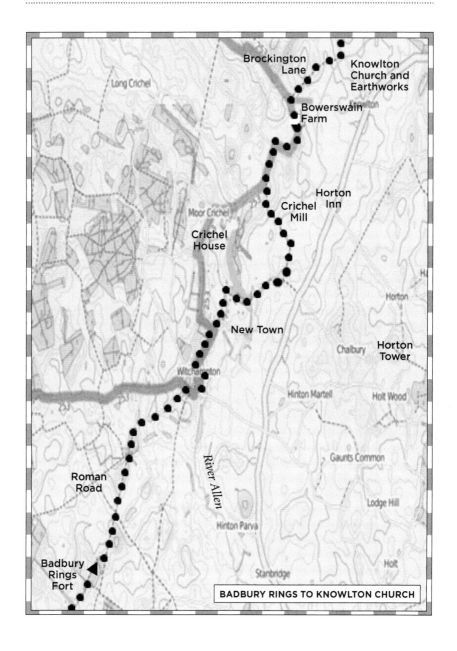

BADBURY RINGS TO KNOWLTON CHURCH

After one-third of a mile leave National Trust land on a grassy track and then a narrow path between hedges. At junction with bridle way continue on path straight ahead until it reaches a T- junction of lanes. Keep straight on past Zannies Cottages to the crossroads and then again to a red brick cottage. Between a cottage and the Wesleyan chapel follow a track right to a line of trees then down on grass to a gate onto lane, where turn left through the village of **Witchampton**. Pass a manor house behind a sixteenth century brick wall and the nineteenth century church of **St Mary, St Cuthberga and All Saints**, built in flint and stone with an impressive lychgate. Witchampton is a live village with its school, community social club and shop with coffee bar. On the right is an Elizabethan cottage dated 1580 and a magnificent yew.

Continue straight ahead on the road to **Moor Crichel**. Just past a cottage which was the old post office pass through an ornate stone archway into the grounds of **Crichel House**. Follow the concrete path, with a sports field on the right and good views ahead to the Palladian mansion, built in the eighteenth century by Humphrey Sturt, who moved the village of Moor Crichel south to **New Town**, near the archway, to create an ornamental lake. He was also interested in farming methods and used an artificial fertiliser made from ash from a London soap factory. There is a private chapel to the right of the house overlooking the lake.

Turn right before a cattle grid to continue down a track with the lake on the left. Pass through a white gate to take the left-hand fork of a track and then on to criss-cross the River Allen to take a track to the left with the river on right which leads to Crichel Mill. Keep straight on uphill on track to a bend from where there is a good view of the **Horton Inn** to the east. Parts of it date back to the early eighteenth century, when it was a post house of the London to Exeter stage coaches. Follow the track to a lane where turn right then quite soon right again. Take the next turning to the left. Horton Tower can be seen back to the south-east, also built by Humphrey Sturt, as an observatory, if only to watch the hunt from in his old age.

The lane leads past **Bowerswain Farm** then over a small bridge. Turn right almost immediately on a good bridleway that bears to the left away from the river. In just over three-quarters of a mile the path joins a grass track where turn left to **Brockington farm**.

BADBURY RINGS

At the time of the Napoleonic Wars **Badbury Rings** was one of a chain of beacons extending over southern England. In *The Trumpet Major* Miller Loveday takes Mrs Garland and Anne to watch King George III review his troops on the downs near Weymouth. It was a clear day and they could see for miles:

> *Inland could be seen Badbury Rings, where a beacon had been recently erected; and nearer, Rainbarrow, on Egdon Heath, where another stood: further to the left Bulbarrow ... Nettlecombe Tout; ...*

This was before the trees were planted on Badbury.

Hardy was familiar with the Dorchester to Salisbury Roman road. He refers to it in *The Return of the Native* and he wrote *The Roman Road:*

> *The Roman Road runs straight and bare*
> *As the pale parting-line in hair*
> *Across the heath. And thoughtful men*
> *Contrast its days of Now and Then,*
> *And delve, and measure, and compare;*
> *Visioning on the vacant air*
> *Helmed legionaries, who proudly rear*
> *The Eagle, and they pace again*
> > *The Roman Road.*
>
> *But no tall brass-helmed legionnaire*
> *Haunts it for me. Uprises there*
> *A mother's form upon my ken,*
> *Guiding my infant steps, as when*
> *We walked that ancient thoroughfare,*
> > *The Roman Road.*

HORTON/LORNTON INN

Barbara of the House of Grebe went to meet her disfigured husband at the **Lornton Inn**, a *solitary wayside tavern ... the rendezvous of many a daring poacher for operations in the adjoining forest*; the scene of their elopement. Agitated and conspicuous when he doesn't arrive, she prepares to hire a conveyance in which to return home when Lord Uplandtowers offers a lift in his carriage.

> *There was not much accommodation for a lady at this wayside tavern; ...*

The route goes left but I recommend a short diversion to the right (half a mile) to see **Knowlton Church and Earthworks** to the left of the lane. The circular earthwork dates from 2500 BC and may have been used for religious purposes by men of the early Bronze Age. What makes the place particularly interesting is that the early Christians built a church right in the centre of the henge, perhaps to counteract the paganism of the place. The ruin that remains was abandoned in the fourteenth century when the village of Knowlton was decimated by the Black Death. There are many Bronze Age round barrows in the area around the earthwork but most have been lost to the plough.

Back at Brockington Farm take the track off to the right at the end of farm buildings past Brockington Cottages. When it crosses several other tracks continue straight with hedge to soon turn right to join a grassy track between fences towards farm buildings; the farmyard end can be very muddy. On the lane turn right into **Wimborne St Giles**, the attractive estate village of the Shaftesbury estate with refreshment available at the **Bull Inn**. Look for seventeenth century **Mill House** on the River Allen with the village stocks opposite and the **Church of St Giles** adjoining seventeenth century almshouses on the village green. The exterior of the church is mainly eighteenth century but the interior was restored by the famous architect Ninian Cooper after a fire in 1908. There are several monuments to the Shaftesbury family; the philanthropic 7th Earl (1801-85), of boy chimney sweep and Eros in Piccadilly Circus fame, is buried here. **St Giles House,** near the church, is the home of the Earls of Shaftesbury. Hidden by trees the battlemented house dates from the sixteenth century.

Leave the village past **The Bull** then right, across the river to a minor road past an elegant manor house on the left. Where a track bisects the lane turn right (also the Jubilee Trail) then at a T- junction go left for a straight quarter-mile until a right turn towards an open barn on the B3081. Follow the footpath sign to the left then right along the lane by **Creech Hill House**. After a further quarter-mile take a footpath on a bend diagonally down across a field to a stile in the direction of Cranborne church. Cross a farm lane to head for the left end of a line of majestic beeches, then follow a well-trodden path across the field into **Cranborne**. Part of this parallels a line of mature poplars and a clipped yew hedge through which is an entrance to and a good view of privately owned **Cranborne Manor** with its superb seventeenth century walled gardens.

she was conscious that more eyes were watching her from the inn-windows than met her own gaze.

The inn has many more windows now since it has doubled in size. It no longer fits the description wayside tavern as it has a large restaurant with a wide menu.

ST GILES HOUSE/KNOLLINGWOOD HALL

The home of Lord Uplandtowers in *Barbara of the House of Grebe*. The gallery in the 'boudoir' where Barbara hides the statue of her dead husband still exists.

CRANBORNE/CHASEBOROUGH

In *Tess of the d'Urbervilles* the **Trantridge** workfolk made a weekly Saturday night pilgrimage to **Chaseborough** a *decayed market-town two or three miles distant;* here they disported themselves at various inns including 'The Flower-de-Luce' and often went on to less well-ordered premises for dancing. On the fateful September evening of her seduction by Alec d'Urberville Tess finds them at a *private little jig at the house of a hay-trusser and peat dealer who lived in an out-of-the-way nook of the townlet.* One of the men explains to Tess:

'*The maids don't think it respectable to dance at the "Flower-de-Luce" … They don't like to let everybody see which be their fancy-men. Besides, the house sometimes shuts up just when their jints begin to get greased'.*

Tess, tired, becomes impatient to return to Trantridge but refuses Alec's offer to 'come to the *"Fleur-de-Luce"* and I'll hire a trap, and drive you home with me.' At a quarter past -eleven Tess leaves with the Trantridge people *straggling along the lane which led up the hill towards their homes.*

Cranborne was the administrative centre of **Cranborne Chase**, a vast royal hunting ground from the time of King John in the thirteenth century until it was ceded to Robert Cecil, Viscount Cranborne and later Earl of Salisbury by James I in the seventeenth century. The manor has been in the Cecil family ever since. Chase laws protected the deer until 1830 but this encouraged deer stealing, poaching and smuggling.

Cranborne's importance as a market town diminished when it was bypassed in the last century by the Great Western turnpike road and then later by the railway. Today it is an attractive village with good accommodation. The large stone and flint church dates from Norman times but is mainly late medieval with some nineteenth century restoration. It contains an unusual memorial to a young boy who died from a fish bone in his throat!

The English Heritage site of Knowlton Church and Rings is a very rare Sacred Circle. A twelfth century stone and flint Norman church in the centre of a Neolithic ritual henge.

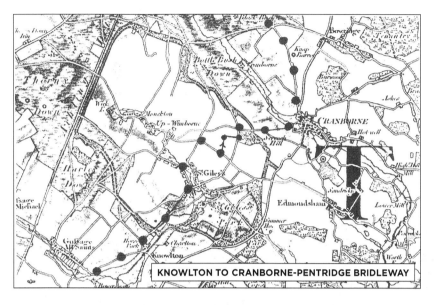

KNOWLTON TO CRANBORNE-PENTRIDGE BRIDLEWAY

An early motor car in Cranborne. In the background is the Fleur de Lys with both a garage and stables. Hardy often went motoring at this time, but never learned to drive, preferring to cycle. Photograph: E. Dodshon, 1916

FROM CRANBORNE TO SHAFTESBURY

This part of the walk passes through some of the most splendid scenery in Dorset and Wiltshire, varying from remote, windswept downs dotted with evidence of prehistoric man, to deep, tranquil coombes where time seems to have been suspended.

Leave **Cranborne** to the north on a minor road from Salisbury Street to Tidpit and Martin. After a quarter-mile take a left fork on a No Through Road, a bridleway to **Pentridge**, some two-and-a-half miles. In bad weather follow it all the way, but in fair conditions I recommend branching off to the right to **Pentridge Hill** and descending via **Penbury Knoll**, once a beacon. About halfway to Pentridge the Jubilee Trail joins the Way from the left. Continue ahead to a gate where the bridleway branches left. If fine continue upwards on the Jubilee Trail towards the pine trees of Penbury Knoll. Enter the knoll through gate where go straight on for a short way to a trig point at the highest point on the left. The views across Cranborne Chase, the Wiltshire Downs and Ringwood Forest are spectacular. The descent to Pentridge is to the left just after the trig point, leaving the Jubilee Trail. You will have to pick your way as there is no clear path. The spire of Pentridge Church is just visible through the trees. Head for this, over a stile down to the edge of a field where, at the end of a wire fence, go on down over a stile to enter the village by a narrow path.

Pentridge is quite near the A354 but is an oasis of tranquillity. To see the church and village green turn right along the lane then left up a track. The cottages are mostly brick and flint while the **Church of St Rumbold**, rebuilt in 1855, is in flint and greensand with a spire. Inside is a memorial plaque to Robert Browning's great grandfather who lived nearby.

Return to the lane to follow it back past the point of entry into the village almost due south until it becomes a muddy track. At a Y junction branch right then bear right uphill along the side of a field. Continue through a gateway up field on bridleway.

CRANBORNE CHASE/THE CHASE

In *Two on a Tower* Hardy describes **The Chase** as seen from the train between Wimborne and Salisbury:

a country of ragged woodland, which, though intruded on by the plough at places, remained largely intact from prehistoric times, and still abounded with yews of gigantic growth and oaks tufted with mistletoe.

In *Tess of the d'Urbervilles* it is :

a truly venerable tract of forest land, one of the few remaining woodlands in England of undoubted primaeval date, wherein Druidical mistletoe was still found on aged oaks, and where enormous yew-trees, not planted by hand of man, grew as they had grown when they were pollarded for bows.

Alec d'Urberville refers to it as the *oldest wood in England* and it is here that he rapes Tess after having 'rescued' her from the *dark virago* Car Darch on the return to Trantridge from Chaseborough. Hardy uses the intensity and paganism of the place to evoke a sense of doom and despair:

Darkness and silence ruled everywhere around. Above them rose the primeval yews and oaks of The Chase …

PENTRIDGE/TRANTRIDGE

Tess took a horse-drawn 'van' which *twice in the week ran from* **Shaston** **(Shaftesbury)** *eastward to Chaseborough, passing near* **Trantridge***,* to call on her newly-discovered, rich relative, Mrs d'Urberville. The Slopes, the d'Urberville mansion, does not exist, but its surroundings closely resemble Pentridge and Cranborne. Hardy describes Trantridge as a place where the inhabitants *drank hard* and scorned the idea of saving money for their old age, preferring the *fuller provision* of parish relief!

OAKLEY DOWN

Hardy was deeply interested in the evidence of prehistoric and Roman Britain in the landscape. In the poem *My Cicely* her former lover speeds westwards from Salisbury to search for her:

I traversed the downland
Whereon the bleak hill-graves of Chieftains
Bulge barren of tree;

This area, **Oakley Down**, is rich in archaeological interest. Directly west is the massive causeway of **Ackling Dyke** Roman road and a variety of Bronze Age burial mounds. The path has just crossed the **Dorset Cursus**, the remains of a Neolithic six mile long monument that consisted of two banks and ditches about a hundred yards apart. About one-and-a-half miles east is **Bokerley Ditch**, an earthwork built in the fourteenth century to defend settlements beside the Roman road from Sarum to Badbury Rings.

The bridleway veers to the right towards buildings on the A354 which is the point where the course of this road joins that of Ackling Dyke. Nearly one-and-a half miles east is Woodyates, where there was a noted inn on the eighteenth century turnpike. George III used it on his journeys between Weymouth and London, but it was superseded by the advent of the railway. In 1919 Hardy was surprised that it had not been re-opened when the motor car increased road traffic. It was demolished in the 1960s.

Cross the road and join bridleway along the side of a field. Bear left at the bottom then straight ahead for just over half a mile to a farm lane with good views back to Penbury Knoll. Cross the lane to follow bridleway which soon bears right downhill in the direction of **Sixpenny Handley** church and the lively village of Sixpenny Handley. At gap between fields keep to the lower field down to track and then lane. Turn right then fork left to **Deanland** — just under a mile past two magnificent beeches, the Barleycorn House, once a public house and some attractive cottages. Just past the telephone kiosk on the left follow a footpath to the left to cross stile and follow edge of wood uphill to stile on left. Ignore this cross footpath to continue ahead to cross field on slight right diagonal to stile hidden in the top left-hand corner of the field. If the field is cropped you can follow its edge to the same point. Cross stile to turn left to gate then cross fields to right of barn soon visible ahead. At farm track/bridleway turn right in direction of extensive woodland. Follow track to enter wood where pheasants are reared and are everywhere. Continue straight ahead for about a quarter mile to crosstracks. You are now on the **Rushmore Estate**, glorious woodland typical of Cranborne Chase. Turn left on major path which is the Shire Rack, the county boundary between Dorset and Wiltshire. The woodland is rich in flora and fauna. Woodland birds include jay, marsh tit, nuthatch, tree creeper and woodpecker. The coppices provide cover for nightingales, turtle doves and warblers. Deer abound.

He returns disillusioned:

Uptracking where Legions had wayfared
By chromlechs unstoried,
And lynchets, and sepultured Chieftains.

WOODYATES/WOODYATES INN

In the collection of stories *Life's Little Ironies* in *A Few Crusted Characters* Mr George Crookhill and his odd travelling companion water their horses at this inn.

THE LARMER TREE GROUNDS, TOLLARD ROYAL

In September 1895 Hardy made a note of a newspaper report of the annual sports at the **Larmer Tree** which he attended with Emma:

'the illumination of the grounds by thousands of Vauxhall lamps, and the dancing of hundreds of couples under these lights and the mellow radiance of the full moon … mostly the polka-mazurka and schottische, though some country dances were started by the house-party, and led off by the beautiful Mrs Grove, the daughter of General Pitt-Rivers, and her charming sister-in-law, Mrs Pitt. Probably at no other spot in England could such a spectacle have been witnessed at any time. One could hardly believe that one was not in a suburb of Paris, instead of a corner in old-fashioned Wiltshire, nearly ten miles from a railway-station in any direction.'

Hardy, always romantically susceptible to beautiful women, danced with Agnes Grove. Many years later, on hearing of her death, he remembered that far-off evening in a poem, *Concerning Agnes*:

I am stopped from hoping what I have hoped before –
Yes, many a time!
To dance with that fair woman yet once more
As in the prime
Of August, when the wide-faced moon looked through
The boughs at the faery lamps of the Larmer Avenue.

This was the last time Hardy danced *on the greensward* as he later got stiff knees!

Follow straight on ignoring all the major tracks that bisect it that have grand names like Oxford Street and Bridmore Ride — elegant but deserted, once used by horse carriages on their way to **Rushmore House**, the former home of the Pitt-Rivers family, where General Augustus Henry Lane-Fox Pitt-Rivers, a renowned archaeologist and anthropologist, entertained Hardy and Emma for several days in 1895. The General created the **Larmer Tree Grounds**, Tollard Royal, in the 1880s for the entertainment of local people and visitors. There were annual sports, theatre, music, dancing and ornamental buildings that Pitt-Rivers acquired from the Indian Exhibition at Earls Court, London, in 1890.

The Larmer Tree was an old wych-elm, now replaced by an oak on the same spot. The gardens were illuminated by thousands of tiny lamps and attracted 44,817 visitors at their peak in 1899.

Today they can be hired for private functions and regular music festivals are held in summer. The gardens and café are open to the public several days a week.

Eventually the path skirts and then emerges on to Rushmore Park Golf Club. Bear right along the edge of course keeping near signs and wary of golf balls! The path skirts the Club buildings to reach a large metal field gate. Follow on through wood to a drive. Cross this and then a field keeping to the right of copse to reach a gate. Continue downhill to further gate and track which leads to the road. Just before reaching this turn right along a track shown on the OS map as **Tinkley Bottom**. Follow this to pass through a substantial gate. Go straight on across two small sloping fields through two more gates towards a dry valley. Soon after the second gate and opposite a fine double iron deer park gate on the right take a footpath to the left steeply uphill between coppices of beech and sycamore. Follow fence through two more gates before descending, with fine views on the right towards **King John's House** and **Tollard Royal Church**. Follow the road carefully into the village.

As its name indicates **Tollard Royal** has royal connections; King John hunted in Cranborne Chase nearly 800 years ago and his hunting lodge, King John's House, near the church, is impressive although altered. It is still the home of descendants of General Pitt Rivers; the family have had

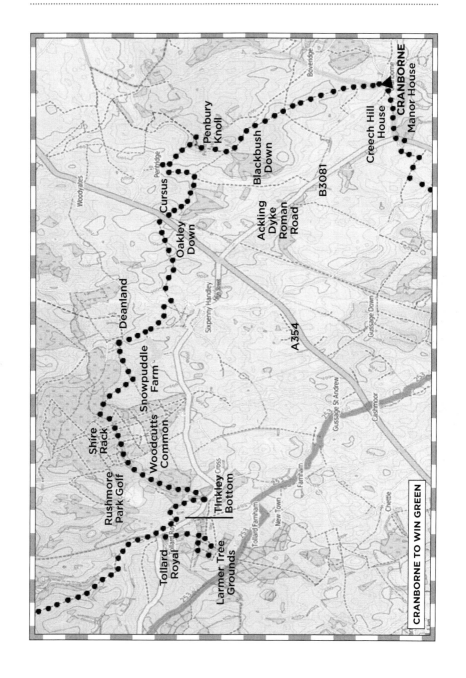

CRANBORNE TO WIN GREEN

associations with The Chase since Elizabethan times. Chase Courts were held here and Rushmore Lodge (as it was then known) was used as an operational headquarters of The Chase from the fifteenth century.

The chancel of the **Church of St Peter ad Vincula** (in chains) dates from the fourteenth century. There is an interesting brass memorial (1865) to a young lady killed by an avalanche while on her honeymoon in the Alps. In the churchyard are some unusual triangular tombstones.

A detour to glimpse the **Larmer Tree Grounds** and imagine their former glories entails a round trip of about one-and-a half miles from the church. Take a path to the left from the lane uphill from the church. Follow between fences to a tall deer gate into a small wood then out to bear right across a field to a dip in the far right corner. On the track fork left to follow a fence round the Larmer grounds until you can get a good view.

Visit the café if open. (Sunday to Thursday 11.a.m. to 4.30p.m.)

The plaintive cries of mating peacocks can be heard from spring to autumn.

A troupe of clowns performing to a gathering in the Larmer Tree Grounds on the Rushmore Estate at Tollard Royal at their peak in 1899. Source:Rodney Legg collection

WIN GREEN/WINGREEN

Wingreen is mentioned in *Tess*. After Alec subjects Tess to a hurtling ride downhill in the dog-cart, as they approach **Melbury Down** and Wingreen, he threatens to repeat the performance. Tess promptly drops her hat as an excuse to dismount and walk the rest of the way to Trantridge. The terrain around Win Green makes this incident easy to imagine.

A poem of seduction and regret *The Vampirine Fair* is also set in this area with mention of Wingreen, the Manor Court (**Rushmore**), **Shastonb'ry** (**Shaftesbury**), and a 'churchyard home' where the church has a steeplecock (**Tollard**).

SHAFTESBURY/SHASTON/SHASTONB'RY

Shaston was the old and economical name for Shaftesbury on milestones.

In *Tess* the town is one of the boundaries of the world for the young Tess gazing from her window in **Marlott** (**Marnhull**):

> *She had seen daily from her chamber-window towers, villages, faint white mansions; above all the town of Shaston standing majestically on its height; its windows shining like lamps in the evening sun.*

In *Jude the Obscure* Hardy describes Shaston in detail, calling it the city of a dream because of its historic interest and *one of the queerest and quaintest spots in England … breezy and whimsical* because of its situation and singularity.

He mentions the difficulty of water supplies in bygone days:

> *… within living memory horses, donkeys and men may have been seen toiling up the winding ways to the top of the height, laden with tubs and barrels filled from the wells beneath the mountain, and hawkers retailing their contents at the price of a halfpenny a bucketful.*

In fact the water originated from a spring in the village of Enmore Green under the northern slope of the town. Shaftesbury had a traditional right to use the spring, confirmed in an annual ceremony.

To return to the pond continue past the main entrance to the gardens to the end of the conifer and laurel hedge where take a footpath to the left close to the perimeter fence. Follow this downhill back to the steep-sided field. Down then up to the edge of the small wood to retrace the route.

Leave the village from the pond. Take the surfaced track to the entrance to a farm then continue on a track between yew hedges next to the farm barn. This leads to a gate: it is now also the Wessex Ridgeway. The path leads through deep coombes that become increasingly wild and remote. Sheep crop the sides of the enfolding hills and hawks hover. At the end of the path go through two gates, turn briefly left (the Wessex Ridgeway goes right), then soon right up hill with hedge on left on a farm track/ public footpath signposted **Win Green**. A relentless uphill slog for nearly a mile reveals sweeping views across to Ashcombe House where Madonna once lived with film director Guy Ritchie. Follow the track up to Win Green, which at 910 feet is the highest hill in Cranborne Chase. To reach the summit with its clump of wind-swept beech trees go through a gate and stile off to the right of the track. Gaze south over The Chase towards the New Forest and the coast, east along the prehistoric ridgeway, the Ox Drove, north over the valley to Whitesheet Hill and the Wiltshire Downs over which the old Shaftesbury to Salisbury turnpike ran, and west to Shaftesbury and the wooded slopes of Duncliffe Hill.

Join the main track beyond the summit to turn left towards the parking area. Take a path off to the right across a stile next to a gate (again the Wessex Ridgeway) follow downhill on a left diagonal alongside a fence towards a wood. Join the lane which is the Bath to Hamworthy Roman road. Turn right then soon left on a bridleway into a wood. Follow straight on to the edge of wood then continue on narrow path to field. Here leave the Wessex Ridgeway, which forks right, to go straight on with bank and then hedge on right to pass through several gates to a path which leads to a lane near the village of **Charlton**. Turn left to pass Manor Farm Cottage on right with its unusual pagoda gateway. Turn right at the cottage up a track to gate. Continue down to a small lake. The path goes straight on between this and nearby watercress beds then between wire up towards a barn. Go straight through Greenacre farmyard to join the A30. Turn right towards the **Grove House Hotel** and cross road to path off left just before the inn through a kissing gate and up steep bank. Continue straight on to

Hardy also recounts:

two other odd facts, namely, that the chief graveyard slopes up as steeply as a roof behind the church, and that in former times the town passed through a curious period of corruption, conventual and domestic which gave rise to the saying that Shaston was remarkable for three consolations to man, such as the world afforded not elsewhere. It was a place where the churchyard lay nearer to heaven than the church steeple, where beer was more plentiful than water, and where there were many more wanton women than honest wives and maids.

The churchyard in question is that of one of the ancient churches now non-existent, **St John's**. The graveyard is perched above a wall on to the road just round a sharp bend at the end of **Bimport** – obviously on a higher level than the church was. It is a lonely and abandoned spot with its spreading yew trees and dilapidated tombstones.

Hardy also mentions that the town was used as a winter resting-place by travelling folk *whose business lay largely at fairs and markets.*

Jude arrives at the nearest station (**Gillingham**) and after a weary climb finds the school where Sue and Richard Phillotson work. While waiting for the children to leave he walks from Bimport along **Abbey Walk**. The school buildings *extensive and stone-built* have now been converted into housing for the elderly. They are best viewed from Abbey Walk, a left turning past Trinity Centre. The *two enormous beeches with smooth mouse-coloured trunks* are sadly gone, the last one having been felled quite recently as it had become dangerous.

Sue tells Jude that they live in *that ancient dwelling across the way called Old-Grove Place* which depresses her because it *is so antique and dismal* and makes her feel *crushed into the earth by the weight of so many previous lives there spent.* The Ox House has since been restored. It juts out onto the pavement.

Jude misses the coach for the station which leaves from the Duke's Arms in the Market Place – the present **Grosvenor Hotel**, an early nineteenth century building named after the Grosvenor family, who used to own most of the town. He returns to look longingly at Sue from the street, having passed through *the venerable graveyard of Trinity Church, with its avenue of limes.* These are still there and the place virtually unchanged.

further gate into a housing estate. Pass through this to **Ludwell County First School** where at main lane turn left then right into a small estate of bungalows. Near the end of this cul-de-sac turn right along a short grassy track between bungalows.

Go straight down the hill in the field to small gate then on to right of cottage and barn to emerge on lane. Turn left along the unspoilt valley of the **Coombe** villages with sheep grazing by a stream — one of the headwaters of the **River Nadder**. At **Middle Coombe** crossroads turn right into a No Through Road into the village, tranquil and mellow, with a productive vegetable garden on the right and a brook. Continue up steep hill opposite, round a bend to go through a bridlegate on left between two other gates. Holly bushes overhang the way initially but soon give way to a pretty path with a valley on left and a wood with chestnut trees on the right. At stile cross fields to gate near cottage.

Turn left then take the second footpath to the right near gate. Cross field with attractive lake on right to turn right on lane and follow to its end to a grassy track into **Long Bottom**, a superb coombe with a clear path ahead to a stile in top right hand corner. The path emerges onto the private road to **St Mary's School**. Turn left for a short distance to where the path goes right by the remnant of a stone wall. Go through wood to field then straight uphill to gate where several fields meet. Continue straight on to gate ahead then cross field on a right diagonal to stile in fence. Follow this lane left into **Shaftesbury**. At the bypass turn right then cross to turn left down Coppice Street into the town centre.

Shaftesbury, an ancient Saxon hilltop town, is my home town and I love it. Tourists often shiver as they search diligently for **Gold Hill**, the Hovis street that climbs steeply from the parish of **St James** under the steep southern slope of the 700 ft high greensand spur on which the town is perched, overlooking the Blackmore Vale. The wind frequently whips along the High Street even on a summer's day. But Shaftesbury is a magical place, steeped in history, but continuing with determination in the twenty-first century with its Thursday market, inviting coffee shops and pubs. There is still one of those old-fashioned department stores where you can buy clothes, soft furnishings, haberdashery and myriad other things, all served with traditional courtesy. To experience the real spirit of the place, however, you

The route along Tinkley Bottom into Tollard Royal

The Ox House was Old-Grove Place, the schoolmaster's house that Sue found oppressive in *Jude the Obscure*. Built c1600 it has been restored since Hardy's day but still juts out onto the pavement.

need certain weather conditions, when, on a bright, clear morning, you can walk along **Park Walk** by the Abbey ruins and see the tips of churches and trees protruding through the mist that hangs over the Blackmore Vale. It's a tall order — you can only hope. Hardy thought that Shaftesbury would become a health resort because of its *bracing air*; it hasn't happened — it's not that sort of place.

More factually, the town is built on 100 ft high slopes on all sides except the north-east, making it ideal for a defended settlement in Saxon times. It has strong associations with King Alfred the Great, who founded a nunnery here for his daughter in the ninth century — (one of my sons is named Alfred). It became a place of pilgrimage when the bones of Edward the Martyr were brought to the nunnery from Corfe Castle, via Wareham, in 979. In the 1930s a lead coffin was discovered containing bones that were possibly his. In the fourteenth century Shaftesbury was the most populous town in Dorset and was one of four royal boroughs in the county, together with Dorchester, Bridport and Wareham, but it declined after the Dissolution when many of its religious establishments were destroyed. Only **St Peter's Church**, in the High Street, survives with medieval masonry. The footings of the abbey church may be seen behind Park Walk, which was laid out in 1753.

The **Town Hall** (1826) is worth looking at from the rear, at the top of cobbled **Gold Hill**, lined on one side with eighteenth century cottages and on the other by the imposing retaining wall of the Abbey, dating from the fifteenth century. There is a fine, small museum here.

In **Bimport**, round the corner from the Grosvenor Hotel, is the Shaftesbury Trinity Centre Trust, a former church, designed by Gilbert Scott in 1840. Further along on the right is the **Ox House**, a fine seventeenth century building, now restored.

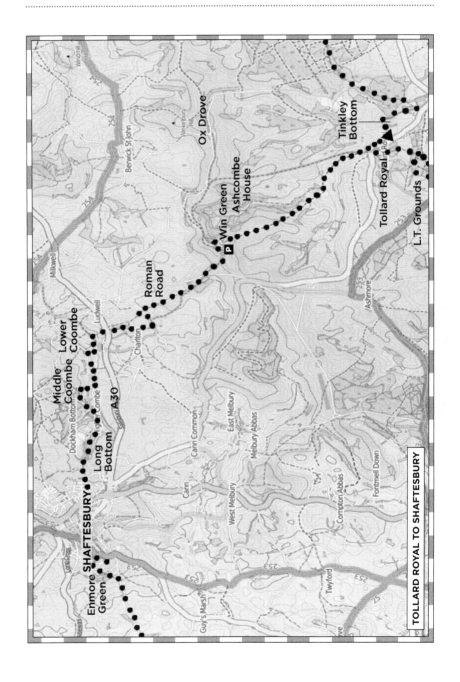

FROM SHAFTESBURY TO STURMINSTER NEWTON

Leave Shaftesbury via Bimport. Just before the Ambulance station, opposite Magdalene Lane, turn right on a path to Castle Hill. Turn left along hill with a wonderful panorama over the Blackmore Vale, Wiltshire and Somerset and ahead Duncliffe Hill, a rounded wooded hummock. Left is a green with picnic facilities, while under the hill nestles the village of **Enmore Green**. Before a kissing gate turn left back to the road where cross the entrance to Castle Gardens to footpath straight ahead which soon descends with beeches on the left. Follow this steeply down to field. The earthworks of a fortress probably founded by King Alfred are on the right. Join lane. Ignore Breach Lane but continue ahead for a short way to footpath to the right across Breach Common. Follow this straight on until it joins a road, Foyle Hill where turn right. If very muddy avoid the footpath and come to the same point by following the narrow lane downhill until it joins Foyle Hill.

The first mile or so from here is on a pleasant minor road, a descent into the **Blackmore Vale**, through which the route passes for nearly twenty miles. Centuries ago this was forest but it is now farming country, a patchwork of fields on heavy soil that makes walking hard work after rain as it can be muddy and flooded from the many meandering streams. Twisting lanes are hemmed in by high hedges, wondrously luxuriant in late spring and early summer when small white umbrellas of cow parsley thicken the grass. There are few hills, but southwards, in the distance, is the ridge of the North Dorset Downs, the sentinels of Okeford Hill, Bulbarrow and Nettlecombe Tout, while to the west Little Minterne Hill and High Stoy mark the end of the Blackmore Vale section of the walk.

Continue down **Foyle Hill** past triangle in lane and on for a good half mile to opposite Thomas's Farm. Take farm track to the right to gate onto hillside meadow. Follow on left diagonal to top corner of field where you enter a nature reserve managed by the Woodland Trust. **Duncliffe Hill** consists of two mounds of greensand covered with mainly deciduous woodland resplendent at bluebell time. Unfortunately it is often very muddy.

BLACKMORE VALE/BLACKMOOR VALE/VALE OF THE LITTLE DAIRIES/FOREST OF THE WHITE HART

A variety of names, but this is above all Tess country, where she spent her childhood and which was *terribly beautiful* to her when she returned from Trantridge. It was the age before motor transport and *The Vale of Blackmoor was to her the world, and its inhabitants the races thereof.* Hardy describes it from the North Dorset Downs:

> *This fertile and sheltered tract of country, in which the fields are never brown and the springs never dry … Here, in the valley, the world seems to be constructed upon a smaller and more delicate scale; the fields are mere paddocks, so reduced that from this height their hedgerows appear a network of dark green threads overspreading the paler green of the grass. The atmosphere beneath is languorous, and is so tinged with azure that what artists call the middle distance partakes also of that hue, while the horizon beyond is of the deepest ultramarine.*

Hardy recalls that in former times the Vale was known as **The Forest of the White Hart**, from a legend that in the thirteenth century a beautiful white hart was killed against Henry III's wishes and a heavy fine imposed on the offender.

Tess trod the road from Shaston to Marlott (Marnhull) when she returned from the d'Urberville mansion – such distances being the norm for pedestrians in those days.

DUNCLIFFE HILL

In *Jude the Obscure* Richard Phillotson walks from Shaston to **Leddenton (Gillingham)**. As he descends into *the low alluvial beds* between the towns, he sees **Duncliffe Hill** on the left. Hardy quotes William Barnes:

> *Where Duncliffe is the travellers mark*
> *And cloty Stour's a-rolling dark.*

The walk soon joins the valley of the River Stour.

MARNHULL/MARLOTT

Marlott features largely in *Tess* as her childhood home and the place to which she returns from time to time in the course of her vicissitudes. The leasehold of the Durbeyfield cottage expires on the death of Tess's father, John, leaving the family

Follow good track ahead and then soon another to left; follow this to a T junction where turn left on undulating track to the south-west tip of wood. Go through gate to follow hedge to gate in top corner of field. To get to this you might have to circumvent farm machinery and nettles! Continue straight ahead to join track to houses and lane.

Continue straight ahead for a few yards on lane to Woodville then take footpath over stile to left over a couple of small fields following a fairly clear path ahead to bridge over ditch into a large field. The path follows a right diagonal but it might be easier to follow border to the right then left until towards the end of field at junction of paths cross double stile through hedge to right. Continue on slight right diagonal down dip, to cross brook and pass right hand end of barns then back towards hunting gate. Through here turn immediately right through big gate with footpath sign. Follow across field to double stile through hedge to left then through field gate straight ahead to next hedge where turn left alongside it. This path exits onto lane at Goods Farm. Cross lane to go straight ahead through farm. Follow concrete track past yurts on left after which the route becomes a grassy track. Follow this into fields to soon curve right with hedge on right and continue along side of several fields until reaching small wooden footbridge in hedge ahead through to lakes. These are part of Todber Manor Fishing Lakes. Pass between the two lakes, through car park to slight uphill track. Follow this to junction of tracks where go straight across to footpath between trees. This emerges to Church Close, **Todber**. Turn right past church and a T junction to take lane to left signposted Fifehead Magdalen to the B3092.

Across the road join a footpath straight ahead alongside hedge. Along the next stretch be careful not to miss stiles partly concealed in hedges! At the end of a small wood on the left continue straight on to a stile. Over this another stile will soon be seen in the hedge on left, cross into field. The right of way continues on a slight left diagonal to reach another rather hidden stile in the hedge ahead. You may have to skirt the field to the right to reach this. Continue straight across the next field to further stile then towards Ashley farm buildings. Keep these on your left to go straight on to end of farm and further gate. With **Marnhull Church** ahead go straight across field, through gate and up side of field to a stile in left-hand hedge where bear right up narrow path to Nash Lane, Pillwell. Soon turn left into the large scattered village of **Marnhull**.

Salisbury Street, Shaftesbury in the winter of 1886. Over 700 feet above sea level, the town experiences severe winters with more than its share of snow. Photograph: Reverend Thomas Perkins

The Crown, Marnhull has a 'pure drop' bar which links it with *Tess*. Marnhill is the largest village in Dorset, described by Hardy as *long and broken*. Drawing: Douglas Snowdon

The village has some very attractive seventeenth and eighteenth century houses and farms. The oldest house **Senior's Farm**, west of the churchyard, which dates from the early sixteenth century with tiny latticed windows and a very large chimney. The fifteenth century tower of the **Church of St Gregory** stands out as a solid landmark across flat, surrounding farmland. The church has several interesting features, including impressive nave and wagon roofs. (Key obtainable at the new rectory opposite Senior's Farm).

Marnhull was once called **Marlhill** because of the white clay or marl found around here which, exposed to air, hardens into the creamy limestone of which many of the buildings are constructed.

In Hardy's time there were two breweries and a malthouse. He visited here in May 1877 for the fortieth anniversary celebrations for Queen Victoria's reign. He also walked from Sturminster Newton and noted the birdsong along the way, the thrushes and blackbirds and the *bullfinch sings from a tree with a metallic sweetness piercing as a fife*.

Leave Marnhull from the **Crown Hotel**. Walk a few yards towards Todber where, opposite a house called The Barn, a footpath enters the farmyard opposite. This passes straight ahead through the farmyard but as gates here are often closed the farmer prefers walkers to bear left round the farm buildings with a slurry pit on left to reach a farm road straight ahead. Follow this down slope and where the road goes left bear right through a gate to follow a generous grass verge straight on and then left to the first stile in hedge to cross a further field in the direction of houses — the next stile is in the left-hand corner of the field and leads to a side lane. Go left for a few yards on the main road before turning left through a small gate into a sloping field. Cross on a left diagonal to the road via a stile in the hedge. Turn left then soon right into Carraway Lane, past impressively clipped yews in a cottage garden, where take path into field on the left. Cross diagonally to the right towards thatched **Tess Cottage** where through gate turn left to cross lane over stile into field where bend back on garden side with good view of cottage. At the end of hedge keep on to cross stiles in hedge ahead then turn left with houses on right.
Go through gate into field to cross more or less straight towards telegraph poles and barns clearly visible on rising ground ahead over the next field. Cross a rather concealed stile in the hedge ahead accessed by a huge lump

homeless. Hardy had strong views about such leases and used *Tess* and other novels to project these. The cottage in question, now called Tess Cottage, can be found to the right of the Marnhull to Sturminster Newton road just north of Walton Elm crossroads and is on the route. It is very well maintained, unlike one imagines the home of the feckless Durbeyfield parents to have been.

The **Pure Drop Inn** which John Durbeyfield tells Pa'son Tringham serves *a very pretty brew in tap – though, to be sure, not so good as at Rolliver's* is the **Crown Hotel**, near the church, which today serves an excellent menu. **Rolliver's**, that disreputable ale-house/off-licence that sold drink on the premises in *a large bedroom upstairs, the window of which was thickly curtained with a great woollen shawl lately discarded by the landlady Mrs Rolliver* is arguably **Old Lamb House**, a solid detached house that stands on the west side of Walton Elm crossroads. For many years its masonry was rendered but it has recently been stripped to the stone beneath – a decided improvement.

The old rectory opposite the church is where Tess pleads with the parson to give her dead child a Christian burial in spite of its unorthodox baptism. The burial takes place in *a shabby corner of God's allotment where He lets the nettles grow,* in the churchyard of **St Gregory's Church**. Nearby is **Marnhull School**, built in 1874, where Tess *passed the Sixth Standard ... under a London-trained mistress.*

The route now leads to Sturminster on paths not far from the river. This was the *back lane* by which Tess returned sadly home from the Vale of Great Dairies after her parting from Angel Clare. She walked towards Marlott via **Cutt Mill** and **Yardgrove Farm**, having left her luggage with the turnpike keeper on the Stourcastle (Sturminster) road.

STURMINSTER NEWTON/STOURCASTLE

The **River Stour** at **Sturminster** was a source of great pleasure to the Hardys:

Rowed on the Stour in the evening, the sun setting up the river ... A fishy smell from the numerous eels and other fish beneath. Mowers salute us. Rowed among the water-lilies to gather them. Their long ropy stems. Passing the island drove out a flock of swallows from the bushes and sedge, which had gone there to roost. Gathered meadow-sweet. Rowed with difficulty through the weeds, the rushes on the border standing like palisades against the bright sky ... A cloud in the sky like a huge quill-pen.

of flat Marnhull stone. The path leads uphill across field towards very large tree. If field is planted follow hedge to the right and then turn left up to the same point. Cross the lane to pass to the left of farm buildings joining the Stour Valley Way. Continue with hedge on left towards clump of trees with good views ahead over the Blackmore Vale to Bulbarrow Hill. Go through two gates by trees, passing pond on right. Follow fence across large field to two gates. In next field turn right down hedge to bottom corner of field then through hedge to turn left along side of field to lane. Turn right.

The ruin of **Cutt Mill** can be seen on the river bank at the bottom of lane. This was once a popular picnic and swimming spot. Back up the lane take the bridleway southwards signposted Wood Lane ¾ mile. At the end of a pleasant deciduous plantation where the track bears left carry straight on through small wood to emerge to a wide bridleway along the side of field. Turn right and follow straight ahead to cross an all weather gallop. Bear right then twice left to pass Wood Lane Stables, Olympic eventer William Fox Pitt's state of the art training establishment. Turn left on the lane then soon right to take a footpath signposted Sturminster Newton. Follow a farm track to wood where bear right and then straight ahead down side of field. Enter thin strip of wood at corner of field, over a tiny brook, to pass through a new kissing gate to open country above the River Stour. An old, half-demolished railway bridge over the river can be seen ahead. The path soon rejoins the Stour Valley way from the right to lead straight ahead into **Sturminster Newton**. This stretch of the route often floods so you may have to branch off left to join the B3092 into the town. In dry conditions you can veer towards the river to view **Colber Bridge**, a white footbridge built in 1841. Hardy enjoyed walking here when he lived with Emma in Riverside Villa from 1876-78. This large Victorian semi-detached stone house is to the left of the path on the edge of the recreation ground in a superb situation high on a cliff overlooking the river. A blue plaque marks the Hardys' occupancy. *The Return of the Native* was written in a first floor room overlooking the river. Hardy later wrote that the years in Sturminster were the happiest of their marriage. They enjoyed the rural atmosphere of the place as a contrast to life in London. In 1916 and again in 1922 Hardy returned to visit Riverside Villa to recall his time here with Emma over forty years before.

Colber Bridge inspired the poem *On Sturminster Foot-Bridge* which Hardy intended to be onomatopoeic:

Reticulations creep upon the slack stream's face
*   When the wind skims irritably past,*
The current clucks smartly into each hollow place
That years of flood have scrabbled in the pier's sodden base;
*   The floating-lily leaves rot fast.*

Hardy's Sturminster poems were written many years after he lived here, but his notebook extracts from the 1870s no doubt recalled images that he was able to use. The poems are especially evocative of the riverside landscape:

The swallows flew in the curves of an eight
*   Above the river-gleam*
*   In the wet June's last beam:*
Like little crossbows animate
The swallows flew in the curves of an eight
*   Above the river-gleam.*

Planing up shavings of crystal spray
*   A moor-hen darted out*
*   From the bank thereabout,*
And through the stream-shine ripped his way;
Planing up shavings of crystal spray
*   A moor-hen darted out.*

Closed were the kingcups; and the mead
*   Dripped in monotonous green,*
*   Though the day's morning sheen*
Had shown it golden and honeybee'd;
Closed were the kingcups; and the mead
*   Dripped in monotonous green.*

These verses are from *Overlooking the River Stour*, which is also a remembrance of Emma.

In June 1877 the celebrations for the fortieth anniversary of Queen Victoria's coronation took place throughout the country. In Sturminster Hardy noted:

… there are games and dancing on the green … The stewards with white rosettes. One is very anxious, fearing that while he is attending to the runners the leg of mutton on the pole will go wrong …

Sturminster Newton, or 'Stur' as it is known locally, is very much a market town. Until 1998 there was a renowned cattle and livestock market. No livestock now but still a lively market on Monday mornings. A fire in 1729 consumed most buildings older than that date but the fifteenth century market cross and thatched market house survived. The Swan was a coaching inn from the eighteenth century. East of the market cross down quiet narrow streets is the **Church of St Mary** which has associations with the Dorset dialect poet, William Barnes, a close friend of Hardy. Barnes was christened here and the lectern is a memorial to him. He also attended school nearby, an attractive cluster of buildings with an ornate entrance, now private homes and the church hall.

The day I visited the church the organist was practising, so I sat beneath the wonderful wagon roof of the nave and let the music wash over me. I came out feeling refreshed, and like Hardy, very much in harmony with Sturminster. In the churchyard is a magnificent giant sequoia; this species is the largest living thing on earth, can live to be over 4,000 years old and grow to a height of nearly 300 feet. This healthy specimen is about 150 years old.

Colber Bridge across the River Stour at Sturminster Newton erected in 1841 by J. Conway, with four stone piers and a parapet of ornamental ironwork. William Barnes crossed it to go to school in Sturminster. Photograph: Sydney S. Carruthers, 1892

Being a countryman Hardy thoroughly approved of country housekeeping skills:

Country life at Stur. Vegetables pass from growing to boiling, fruit from the bushes to the pudding, without a moment's halt, and the goosberries that were ripening at noon are in the tart an hour later.

In *Tess* **Stourcastle** is on the route taken by the young Tess and her small brother Abraham when they transport the beehives from Marlott to Casterbridge (Dorchester). In the early hours of the morning they pass *the little town of Stourcastle, dumbly somnolent under its thick brown thatch.*

STURMINSTER MILL

Towards the end of his life Hardy wrote a poem recalling a visit to **Sturminster Mill** with Florence during their visit to Sturminster in 1916. It is a double memory; the woman on the bridge in the middle verse is Florence, but his memories of Emma from over forty years before dominate the rest of the poem, which must have been extremely irritating to Florence!

THE SECOND VISIT

Clack, clack, clack, went the mill-wheel as I came,
And she was on the bridge with the thin hand-rail,
And the miller at the door, and the ducks at mill-tail;
I come again years after, and all there seems the same.

And so indeed it is: the apple-tree'd old house,
And the deep mill-pond, and the wet wheel clacking,
And a woman on the bridge, and white ducks quacking,
And the miller at the door, powdered pale from boots to brows.

But it's not the same miller whom long ago I knew,
Nor are they the same apples, nor the same drops that dash
Over the wet wheel, nor the ducks below that splash,
Nor the woman who to fond plaints replied, 'You know I do!'

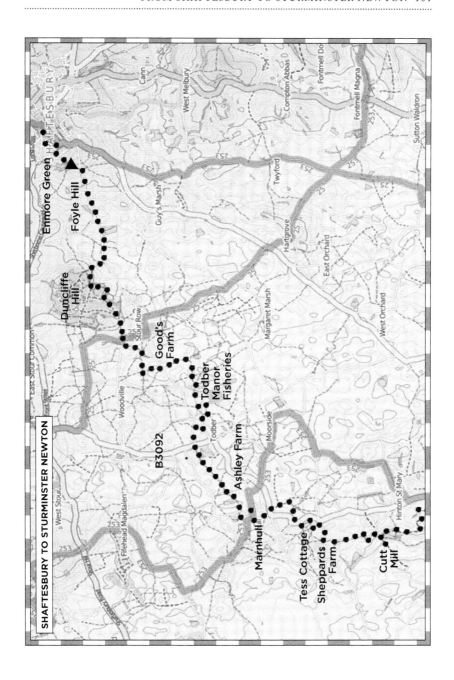

The old market place in Sturminster Newton. The modern market is held just round the corner to the left of the Shaftesbury road. Source: Rodney Legg collection

Sturminster Newton Bridge on a frosty afternoon. Built in the early sixteenth century with six arches, the bridge displays a plaque from the nineteenth century threatening felons with transportation to Australia.

FROM STURMINSTER NEWTON TO BUCKLAND NEWTON

Return to Riverside Villa to resume the path to **Sturminster Mill**. Soon a stone bridge can be seen to the left which dates from the sixteenth century. The mill is one of the few remaining watermills in Dorset; it was repaired and restored by the Mill Trust in 1981.

It is open to the public on Saturday, Sunday, Monday and Thursday from Easter to the end of September from 11a.m. to 5p.m.

Cross the **River Stour** by way of the five hatches, weir and millstream. Alternatively, in muddy conditions, leave the town via Bridge Street to take the last turning to the left, Church Lane, onto the Coach Road, a surfaced path that rejoins the road near the bridge. Cross to pavement, over bridge, then turn right for the Mill.

Join the A357 beyond the mill through **Newton**, an agreeable appendage to Sturminster. Follow the main road towards Sherborne for about one-third of a mile to **Rolls Mill Bridge** where there is a footpath signpost to Puxey Farm. The path originally followed the stream for a short distance but the bank has subsided and the safest option is to go up the drive to pass to the right of the large red brick house (built in 1990). The owner prefers this option to walkers going through the horse paddocks. Go through a gate past the house to cross a field uphill (this section of the path is dependent on where the paddock boundaries are at the time). Past two trees cross stile a short way to the left of a large tree, where bear right down to a footbridge over the Divelish River, a tributary of the Stour. Go through the farmyard of Puxey Farm and then turn left in the first field to head for a bridlegate gap in the hedge straight ahead parallel with the stream you have just crossed. Cross the next two fields to a road and the drive to **Plumber Manor**, an elegant restaurant. The Jacobean house is built from local stone and has been in the Prideaux-Brune family for nearly four hundred years. They manage the restaurant and have converted a stone

HAZELBURY BRYAN/NUTTLEBURY

Tess passes through **Nuttlebury** on two crucial occasions. She parts from Angel Clare at a crossroads between here and Stourcastle and she passes again in the night when she returns home to help her sick parents when summoned from Flintcomb-Ash (Plush) by her sister, Liza-Lu:

At Nuttlebury she passed the village inn, whose sign creaked in response to the greeting of her footsteps, which not a human soul heard but herself. Under the thatched roofs her mind's eye beheld relaxed tendons and flaccid muscles, spread out in the darkness beneath coverlets made of little purple patchwork squares …

The **Antelope** is still a sleepy sort of place not greatly changed from how it was in Hardy's day.

One of Hardy's notebooks contains an extract from the *Dorset County Chronicle* of 28 May 1829 about a man who lived near Hazelbury who had:

a reputation for curing, in a miraculous manner, the King's evil, at his yearly fair or fete. Exactly 24 hours before the new moon in month of May every year, whether it happens by night or day, the afflicted assemble at the doctor's residence, where they are supplied by him with the hind legs of a toad enclosed in a small bag (accompanied with some verbal charm or incantation) and also a lotion and salve of the doctor's preparation. The bag is worn suspended from the neck …

The King's evil was scrofula, tuberculosis of the lymphatic glands. Such beliefs were not uncommon in rural England well beyond 1829. It was not inappropriate that Hardy wrote of the **Blackmore Vale**:

The harts that had been hunted here, the witches that had been pricked and ducked, the green-spangled fairies that 'whickered' at you as you passed; – the place teemed with beliefs in them still, and they formed an impish multitude now.

When Tess returns to Marlott from Flintcomb-Ash she travels to Hazelbury along the ridge of hills to the east of Plush including **Nettlecombe Tout** and **Bulbarrow**. This is certainly not the shortest route as the crow flies, but perhaps *the five miles on the upland* were less arduous than walking the whole distance on the *heavy clay land* in an area of the Blackmore Vale *to which turnpike roads had never penetrated.*

barn to accommodation. Where the drive reaches the stone pillars that are the entrance to the manor fork right on a bridleway to cross a bridge and pass the accommodation area to cross a small grassy area beyond a beech hedge on the right to a footpath (rather overgrown in places).

Cross several fields closely parallel with the **Divelish**. At one point the path goes into a small coppice on the river bank. Emerge on a lane at a stone pack-horse bridge which has two pointed arches and dates back to medieval times. Turn right into **Fifehead Neville**, named after its Doomsday assessment — five hides. Continue for half a mile, past the **Church of all Saints**, much restored since the fourteenth century. In the churchyard is a large eighteenth century tomb of the Brune family. Continue on lane for about one quarter of a mile to take a footpath to left just before a bungalow with conservatory on right. Cross field alongside hedge to gate then turn right to go straight on to another gate from which take a left diagonal to a visible gap in the hedge. Follow the path, keeping always slightly left but forward through a number of gaps, gates and stiles to eventually cross a footbridge over a ditch and pass through a small copse into the bottom of a long field. At the top right two barns can be seen and the path joins a lane to the left of these. Cross this to follow a rough lane then turn left into **Kingston**. At a fork go left and follow the lane round bends. On a sharp left-hand bend take second footpath diagonally down field to Hazel Wood, a Woodland Trust Reserve, where bear left to road then right into Hazelbury Bryan.

Opposite the **Antelope** public house take the footpath alongside a children's play area to a gate, then cross a field slightly to the left to two gates in hedge. Cross another field to more gates then follow straight on main path to eventually bisect track and head uphill towards house to join track and surfaced lane into Wonston. Cross the road to take a No Through Road straight ahead near bus stop. At the end turn sharp left down behind houses into a plantation. Follow on down to cross a small stream then straight on past water trough and gate into large field. Bear left towards bridlegates in bottom right-hand corner of field. Continue parallel with the stream to a stile in the corner, then on by stream until crossing at double bridlegates to a bridlegate ahead. Soon turn sharp left down a path between fence and hedge to a lane. If the path is horribly overgrown cross stream and walk parallel to it to gate to lane. Turn right for half a mile into

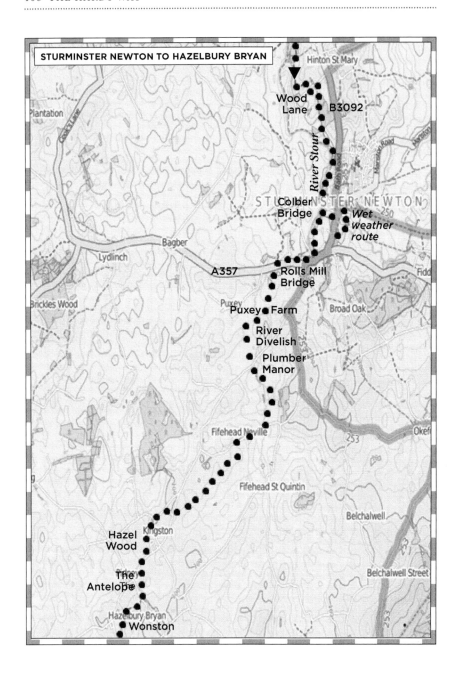

STURMINSTER NEWTON TO HAZELBURY BRYAN

Mappowder. One stretch of this lane is hedged with feathery, ornamental pampas grass — most unusual in a country hedgerow.

Behind the village hall cross the field, to the fifteenth century restored church of **St Peter and St Paul**. The novelist T.F.Powys lived in the single storey stone cottage by the church gate and is buried in the churchyard. His grave is marked by a stone cross near the road. Turn left and pass the Old Rectory, which has most imposing gates with griffons. Continue on the lane to a farm lane on the left where take a footpath near the corner which runs parallel with the lane for nearly half a mile before it emerges just before a farm on the other side of the lane. (You can walk this distance on the lane if you prefer.) Continue on the lane for about one-and-a quarter miles to the **Old Fox** at **Folly**.

Now at last the route leaves the Blackmore Vale which, beautiful though it may be, is not, the best walking country! In fact it's a relief to face the prospect of climbing a hill! There, is, however, a choice of route here. Option One is to climb from Folly to **Church Hill** to avoid further road walking and then to divert back down to **Plush** from the ridge. This means having to retrace your steps up again for about a mile or to continue on to **Henley** without visiting Plush — a pity I think. Option Two is to continue on the lane for a further one-and-a-quarter miles to Plush and to climb Church Hill from there — more direct but entailing more continuous road work; it depends on your time and inclination.

OPTION ONE

Turn right at the Old Fox to climb a bridleway towards **Alton Pancras**. This leads up to the chalk downs via **Ball Hill** to **Church Hill**. The way is well-defined and passes a dew-pond and a prehistoric earthwork enclosure on the left. In season the hillside is bright with gorse. There are excellent views back to the Dorsetshire Gap and Nettlecombe Tout. Follow path straight on until it becomes a track. At a barn on the right is where the path leads back down to Plush. This is not waymarked. Opposite the barn go through gate on left and bend back sharply through a second gate to follow fence to hedge and gate on far side of field. Bear slightly left across a further field to find a small bridlegate in long hedge just over half way along. This emerges into gorse bushes on the side of Watcombe Plain.

PLUSH/CHURCH HILL/FLINTCOMB-ASH

Tess first sees **Flintcomb-Ash** from the hills to the west when she arrives from Port Bredy (Bridport). There is an immediate impression of bleakness and austerity:

> *Here the air was dry and cold, and the long cart-roads were blown white and dusty within a few hours after rain. There were few trees, or none, those that would have grown in the hedges being mercilessly plashed down with the quickset by the tenant-farmers, the natural enemies of tree, bush, and brake.*

She descends into *the remains of a village* and at the entrance is a cottage whose gable jutted into the road. This is easily identifiable in **Plush**. Tess warmed herself on the gable end which reflected the heat of the fire within *that cheered any lonely pedestrian who paused beside it.*

Flintcomb-Ash farm was a *starve-acre place.* **Church Hill** was bleak and bare without the trees and grass that clothe it today. There were vast swede-turnip fields, some of

> *a hundred odd acres, in one patch, on the highest ground of the farm, rising above stony lanchets or lynchets – the outcrop of siliceous veins in the chalk formation, composed of myriads of loose white flints in bulbous, cusped, and phallic shapes.*

Tess and Marian had to grub out the lower half of turnips that had been half eaten by live-stock:

> *Every leaf of the vegetable having already been consumed, the whole field was in colour a desolate drab; it was a complexion without features, as if a face, from chin to brow, should be only an expanse of skin. The sky wore, in another colour, the same likeness; a white vacuity of countenance with the lineaments gone. So these two upper and nether visages confronted each other all day long, the white face looking down on the brown face, and the brown face looking up at the white face, without anything standing between them but the two girls crawling over the surface of the former like flies.*

The weather deteriorates:

> *There had not been such a winter for years. It came on in stealthy and measured glides, like the moves of a chess-player. One morning the few lonely trees and the thorns of the hedgerows appeared as if they had put off a vegetable for an animal integument. Every twig was covered with a white nap as of fur grown*

Bear right down the hill to a gate clearly visible at the tip of a wood. Continue down to a track which emerges onto a lane. Turn left for a few yards to **The Brace of Pheasants**, a good place for refreshments.

If you choose to bypass Plush continue past the barn on the top track with hedge on right until the path forks — leave main track to continue straight ahead down side of field past farm waste. At gateway go straight down on a narrow sunken track — Crowthorne Lane — which soon joins a lane. Turn left for a few yards to take a short footpath on the right to farm buildings on the B3143. Turn right on road then fork left to Henley then after half a mile into **Buckland Newton**, where there is accommodation and a pub called **The Gaggle of Geese**.

OPTION TWO

Follow the lane from Folly to Plush. The little nineteenth century church on the edge of the hamlet is now happily a community centre. Just past the **Brace of Pheasants** find a chalk track leading uphill. As you climb there are good views down to Plush, nestling under the hill and across to the Dorsetshire Gap and Nettlecombe Tout. When the bridleway forks keep straight on. Once you have gone through the gate onto the Access land of Watcombe Plain look out for a stone plinth with a blue arrow half left. This indicates your direction to the gate half left towards the hedge at the top. Soon bear slightly left uphill keeping left towards hedge behind gorse bushes to a small wooden bridlegate. Through gate keep ahead on a slight right diagonal to field gate to next field where follow the fence towards the barn referred to in Option One. Follow route into **Buckland Newton** as described above.

Sheep Grazing above Buckland Newton. Photograph: Arthur Simmonds, 2014

from the rind during the night, giving it four times its usual stoutness; the whole bush or tree forming a staring sketch in white lines on the mournful gray of the sky and horizon. Cobwebs revealed their presence on sheds and walls where none had ever been observed till brought out into visibility by the crystallising atmosphere, hanging like loops of white worsted from salient points of the out-houses, posts, and gates.

Migrating birds arrive from the north *gaunt spectral creatures with tragical eyes* and the frost gives way to snow.

Then one day a peculiar quality invaded the air of this open country. There came a moisture which was not of rain, and a cold which was not of frost. It chilled the eyeballs of the twain (Tess and Marian), made their brows ache, penetrated to their skeletons, affecting the surface of the body less than its core. They knew that it meant snow, and in the night the snow came.

In one of his later collections of poems, *Winter Words*, Hardy included *We Field-Women*, a poem that reflects the conditions he describes in *Tess* and shows his concern for the harsh working conditions of women agricultural workers in the nineteenth century.

How it rained
When we worked at Flintcomb-Ash,
And could not stand upon the hill
Trimming swedes for the slicing-mill.
The wet washed through us – plash, plash, plash:
How it rained!

How it snowed
When we crossed from Flintcomb-Ash
To the Great Barn for drawing reed,
Since we could nowise chop a swede. –
Flakes in each doorway and casement-sash:
How it snowed!

BUCKLAND NEWTON/NEWLAND BUCKTON

In *The Woodlanders* Dr Fitzpiers hears the clock of **Newland Buckton** strike twelve while his horse is drinking at **Lydden Spring**. This is the River Lydden that rises here to flow into the Stour north of Sturminster Newton.

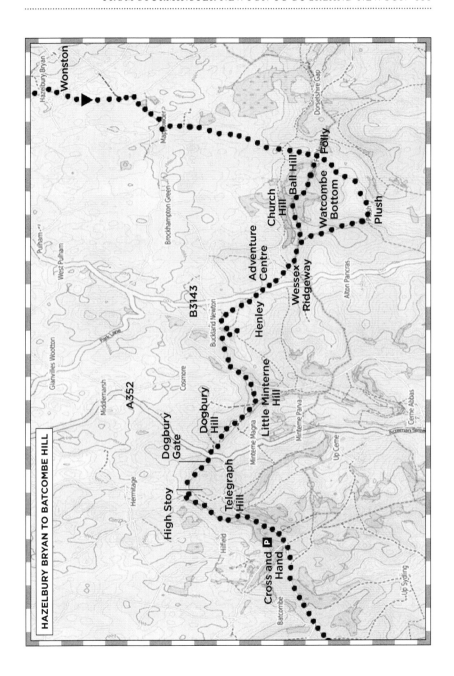

LITTLE MINTERNE HILL TO EVERSHOT/EVERSHEAD

The route now coincides with Tess's abortive journey from Flintcomb-Ash to Emminster (Beaminster) to seek out Angel's parents. She passed *above the Hintocks*: in this context **Minterne Magna** and **Hermitage**, the Hintocks of the later editions of *The Woodlanders*, when Hardy moved the setting to east of the Melburys as a matter of diplomacy, not wanting to offend Lord Ilchester of Melbury House by the implication of association with the questionable character of Mrs Charmond of Hintock House.

Tess then crosses *at right-angles the high-road from Sherton-Abbas (Sherborne) to Casterbridge, and skirting Dogbury Hill and High Stoy, with the dell between them called 'The Devil's Kitchen'*, she continues to **Cross-in-Hand**, across the Roman road called **Long-Ash Lane** (now the A37) and so down into Evershead. Her journey was fifteen miles each way, in winter conditions, *with the ground ringing under her feet like an anvil* at four o'clock in the morning after a hard black frost, to her return late the same day, exhausted and desperately disappointed.

DOGBURY GATE

On a somewhat lighter note is the poem *Life and Death at Sunrise* (Near Dogbury Gate, 1867) – thoughts on the transitory nature of human life. A waggoner and a horseman meet early one morning at **Dogbury Gate**:

With a shouldered basket and flagon
A man meets the one with the waggon,
And both men halt of long use.
'Well,' the waggoner says, 'what's the news?'
– 'Tis a boy this time. You've just met the doctor trotting back,
She's doing very well. And we think we shall call him "Jack".'

'And what have you got covered there?'
He nods to the waggon and mare.
'Oh, a coffin for old John Thinn:
We are just going to put him in.'
'– So he's gone at last. He always had a good constitution.'
'– He was ninety-odd. He could call up the French Revolution.'

FROM BUCKLAND NEWTON TO EVERSHOT

Leave Buckland from the **Church of the Holy Rood** which is rendered — unusual for a Dorset church. It is much more attractive inside than out with a thirteenth century chancel, some good windows and an interesting sixteenth century poor-box. Nearby is the Georgian vicarage. Make for a thatched cottage some way along the road south-west of the church. Just past this turn right up track past cottages. Nearby is the old village pound marked by a sycamore tree. Go through gate to take bridleway that leads straight ahead, not the one that turns right. Cross field then turn right up farm track. Follow this uphill until about ten yards from the road at top branch left to gate. This is a permissive path — follow through gate and keeping parallel to hedge on right soon go through gate to road. Cross to track directly opposite and branch round to the right to a ridgeway on **Little Minterne Hill**. There are fine panoramic views along this ridge, especially back across the Blackmore Vale towards Duncliffe Hill and Shaftesbury and down into the sheltered valley of the River Cerne. High Stoy Hill is opposite and Minterne Magna, with Minterne House, formerly a home of the Churchill family, can be seen nestling in its beautiful gardens with parkland and lake. Near where the track bears right a high bank on the right of the path was once the boundary of a deer park. Pass windswept trees down **Dogbury Hill** for about a mile to the A352 at **Dogbury Gate**, a name that derives from when this was a turnpike road. In 1922 Hardy motored here on two occasions and walked to the top of **High Stoy Hill**, the last time that he was able to climb what was certainly one of his favourite Dorset hills. Cross to lane immediately opposite and follow around High Stoy Hill for three-quarters of a mile through pleasant wood to a bend. Ignore first path off left through trees, just before bend, but take next path left into field. Follow straight ahead keeping Little Coppice on your right through two gates and fields until emerging on hillside where follow the contours of the hill parallel with wood to track (muddy after rain), through mixed woodland of oak, ash, alder and hazel, up **Telegraph Hill** to road. The heavy clay soil of the Blackmore Vale is behind; the chalk uplands of the North Dorset Downs ahead. The Quantocks and the

HIGH STOY HILL

The hills often keep their real names in Hardy's work. In *The Woodlanders* Grace discovers her husband, Fitzpiers,

leaning over a gate on High-Stoy Hill … which opened on the brink of a declivity, slanting down directly into White-Hart or Blackmoor Vale, extending beneath the eye at this point to a distance of many miles.

He was gazing south-east towards Middleton Abbey (Milton Abbas) and Mrs Charmond. Later he travels this route:

through the gorgeous autumn landscape of White- Hart Vale, surrounded by orchards lustrous with the reds of apple-crops, berries and foliage, … the hedges were bowed with haws and blackberries; acorns cracked underfoot, and the burst husks of chestnuts lay exposing their auburn contents as if arranged by anxious sellers in a fruit- market.

Such was the outlook from **High-Stoy**.

CROSS-AND-HAND/CROSS-IN-HAND

This is important in *Tess*. She passes it with Alec on her return journey from Emminster:

Of all spots in the bleached and desolate upland this was the most forlorn… The place took its name from a stone pillar which stood there, a strange rude monolith, from a stratum unknown in any local quarry, on which was roughly carved a human hand.

Alec makes her swear that she will never tempt him from his new-found religious life. Tess is only too glad to make this oath but soon discovers that the pillar is not a Holy Cross, but:

a thing of ill-omen … put up in wuld times by the relations of a malefactor who was tortured there by nailing his hand to a post and afterwards hung. The bones lie underneath. They say he sold his soul to the devil, and that he walks at times.

Cross-in-Hand is also the subject of the poem *The Lost Pyx* – A Mediaeval Legend – which begins:

Some say the spot is banned: that the pillar Cross-and-Hand
Attests to a deed of hell;
But of else than of bale is the mystic tale
That ancient Vale- folk tell.

Mendips in Somerset can be seen behind to the north-west. Turn right for a mile past **Hilfield Hill** picnic site and viewpoint to **Cross and Hand.** This strange stone pillar, also known as Crossy-Hand and Christ-in-Hand, stands in the grass verge on the right of the road just under a quarter of a mile past a turning to Hilfield. Its origin is unknown; it might be a Saxon boundary stone or it could be Roman, perhaps from a temple. Its isolated situation and odd appearance have given rise to several local legends. Hardy and Florence came here on a motoring trip in September 1914 on such a clear day that it was possible to see both the Bristol and English Channels.

Stay on the quiet and open road for a further one-and-a quarter miles. There is a dew pond in a field on the left just past the end of White's Wood. Opposite two lanes off to left, take unmarked byway to the right across field on a left diagonal heading to the right of pair of trees on skyline to gate. Continue with hedge on right to further gate from which descend on an enclosed track with outstanding views towards Somerset. When track becomes a lane pass two cottages and turn left through a gate with signpost into a field just before the third cottage. Follow with hedge on right to hamlet of **Redford** through three fields and a muddy farmyard. (It may be possible to avoid this by turning right directly into lane).

To the left is **Woolcombe Farm**. Hardy believed that his ancestors once owned Woolcombe House, of which nothing now remains except some building material incorporated into the farm buildings. Hardy walked here from Evershot in 1888 but was disillusioned by the fact that his family had lost status since Woolcombe days: *So we go down, down, down*.

Bubb Down, another of Hardy's favourite places, dominates the view ahead to the left. Turn left then immediately right towards **Melbury Bubb**. If conditions are wet and muddy follow the lane northwards to Hell Corner where fork left into the village. Alternatively pass the second cottage to cross stile on left to head due west down into dip, over a small brook, up the other side and across field towards left-hand gate ahead. Soon head for the white 'Look and Listen' sign of the railway crossing on the Dorchester to Yeovil line. Cross this then bear right towards Bubb Down towards a clump of isolated trees where about halfway up the field a short but very muddy track leads off straight ahead to Melbury Bubb. Initially

The tale is of a monk who is called out one night in a storm to administer the last sacraments to a dying man. On his way he drops the pyx containing the Blessed Sacrament. In *dolorous dread* he searches for it then sees a clear straight ray of light shining on the hill. He finds the pyx surrounded by a circle of *common beasts and rare* mesmerised by its sanctity. He administers the last rites to the man in *the cot on the waste* and later erects the stone

> *to mark where shone*
> *That midnight miracle.*

MELBURY BUBB/LITTLE HINTOCK

In *The Woodlanders* **Little Hintock** is described to the barber searching for it as *such a little small place that, as a town gentleman, you'd need to have a candle and lantern to find it if ye don't know where 'tis.*

All the dwellings in Little Hintock are fictional but the setting closely resembles **Melbury Bubb** and **Stockwood**.

> *At length could be discerned in the dusk, about half a mile to one side, gardens and orchards sunk in a concave, and, as it were, snipped out of the woodland. From this self-contained place rose in stealthy silence tall stems of smoke, which the eye of imagination could trace downward to their root on quiet hearthstones, festooned overhead with hams and flitches.*

BUBB DOWN

The wooded country between Melbury Bubb and Melbury Osmond is reminiscent of how large tracts of this area were in the nineteenth century, when the landscape was more thickly wooded than it is today. It was the domain of the cider-maker, the timber, bark and copse-ware merchant, and the spar-maker as exemplified in *The Woodlanders* by Giles Winterborne, George Melbury and Marty South's father, John. Hardy's descriptions sensitively evoke the sylvan atmosphere. Melbury and his daughter, Grace, walk through the woods:

> *They went noiselessly over mats of starry moss, rustled through interspersed tracts of leaves, skirted trunks with spreading roots whose mossed rinds made them like hands wearing green gloves; elbowed old elms and ashes with great forks, in which stood pools of water that overflowed on rainy days and ran down their stems in green cascades. On older trees still than these huge lobes of fungi grew like lungs.*

follow the side of the hill and hedge towards farmyard but then go through the second gate up into another field, turn right to follow hedge to a stile to the right of the barn and another down into the farmyard. Turn left, then right into the tiny village.

The word 'Bubb' derives from the Bubb family once local landowners. The village seems a world apart from the hustle and bustle of the twenty-first century but in reality the busy A37 is only half a mile away. There is a stone manor house, mostly Jacobean, next to the **Church of St Mary the Virgin**, with its avenue of tall yews and fifteen century tower. The church was largely restored in 1854, but has a Saxon font and is still lit by oil lamps.

Where lane ends near church follow track left round corner of wall. Keep right of barns to go through gate and up hill. Turn right after second gate above a quarry near line of majestic beeches, resplendent in autumn glory as I passed. Initially follow fence line but soon bear off left to Trig point and top of steep slope to curving track which leads down steeply to stile at lower left bottom corner of field. Follow muddy path with footbridges and boardwalk to follow track through **Stock Wood** — two deer bounded by as I passed — across a field to reach Church Farm, **Stockwood**. a tiny place with the smallest church in Dorset, fifteenth century and dedicated to the Saxon Saint Edwold, usually left open or the key obtainable from the farmhouse. Cross bridge into field to follow farm drive to road where turn right and then take footpath over stile in hedge on left. Follow hedge on right to further stile to continue along left hand side of next field. The farm on the right is **Manor Farm** once the home of Hardy's mother, Jemima, where she lived with her mother and siblings after their father's death. Cross stile in hedge on left to bear diagonally over field or follow headland round field if there is a standing crop to double stiles and bridge over stream. Continue on left diagonal to gate in far corner beside the **Rest and Welcome Inn** a good refreshment point, on the A37, which follows the course of the old Roman Road from Dorchester to Ilchester and Bath.

Cross the road carefully to continue northwards until stile in hedge. Over this follow hedge on left until crossing line of oak trees, once an old field boundary. Bear slightly right to the farthest right corner of this long field to a gate near cottage garden. Turn right onto concrete track then left along lane, over bridge and uphill past thatched cottages towards the

MELBURY OSMOND/GREAT HINTOCK/KING'S HINTOCK

In the collection of short stories *A Changed Man*, **Monmouth Cottage** at **Townend** is the setting for *The Duke's Reappearance*. Christopher Swetman (this is the real surname of Hardy's ancestors) lived here in a house with mullioned windows on the *outskirts of King's Hintock village*. He shelters a mysterious stranger later believed to be the Duke of Monmouth fleeing after the battle of Sedgemoor. The Duke assists with the domestic duties of the household by fetching water from **Buttock's Spring** – the brook crossed on the path into **Melbury Osmond** just before Town's End. Next day he leaves by **Clammer's Gate** across the park to Evershead. Tradition has it that there is truth in this tale.

Another short story *Interlopers at the Knap* in *Wessex Tales* is also set in Melbury Osmond,

> *one of the Hintocks. where the people make the best cider and cider-wine in all Wessex, and where the dunghills smell of pomace instead of stable refuse as elsewhere.*

Sally Hall and her mother live in:

> *an old house with mullioned windows of Ham-hill stone, and chimneys of lavish solidity. It stood at the top of a slope beside King's-Hintock village-street, only a mile or two from King's-Hintock Court … Immediately in front of it grew a large sycamore tree, whose bared roots formed a convenient staircase from the road below to the front door of the dwelling. Its situation gave the house what little distinctive name it possessed, namely, 'The Knap'. Some forty yards off a brook dribbled past, which, for its size, made a great deal of noise.*

This more or less equates with **Manor Cottage**, on the left on the lane up to the church. The remains of a large yew (not a sycamore) can be seen on the bank near the house.

The poem *One Who Married Above Him* also mentions this house. It is a bitter tale of a man who leaves his wife and children because he is humiliated by the wife's perpetual feeling that she has married beneath her:

> *And there stands the house, and the sycamore-tree and all,*
> *With its roots forming steps for the passers who care to call,*
> *And there are the mullioned windows, and Ham-Hill door,*
> *Through which Steve's wife was brought out, but which Steve*
> *re-entered no more.*

church. Jemima Hardy was born and spent her childhood, one of seven children in poor circumstances, in 1, Barton Hill Cottages, thatched, on the left at the top of the hill. Hardy's grandmother, Elizabeth Swetman of this village, had married George Hand of Affpiddle – now Affpuddle – *a young man of whom her father strongly disapproved*. Past the cottage and old red telephone kiosk turn left at bus shelter across gravelled drive to enter churchyard.

The **Church of St Osmond** rebuilt in 1745, having become ruinous, was restored again in 1888. Jemima Hardy was baptised and married here; her marriage certificate can be seen on the wall.

Leave the churchyard via the impressive avenue of yews to go south along main village street. It is sad to note the demise of former village institutions in the name of the cottages, now private residences: The Old Rectory, The Old Post House, Chapel Cottage. A cottage on the left is called Little Hintock from Hardy's *The Woodlanders*. Pass through the water splash. After left hand bend at **Town's End** is **Monmouth's Cottage**, once the home of Hardy's maternal ancestors with its great wooden front door and warm thatch. Hardy noticed the loss of stone chimneys and an oak staircase when he visited the village.

Follow lane round to the **Clammer's Gate** entrance to **Melbury Park** and **House**, also known as **Melbury Sampford**. The estate road leads completely straight through gracious parkland with sheep grazing among mature trees. The house is huge and of varying dates, the earliest Elizabethan. It has been the seat of the Strangways family, the Earls of Ilchester, for about five hundred years. Best viewed from the Evershot side across the lake, the gardens are sometimes open to the public but the house and fifteenth century church on the east side seldom so. Bear right to follow the road through the deer park, where there are three species of deer: red, fallow and sika. Pass through **Lion Gate**, to arrive in Evershot and the **Acorn Inn**, for refreshment and accommodation.

Tess Cottage, of cob and thatch, next to the church of **St Osmund** (again!), stands right on the road as do the church and inn. In Back Lane, between the church and Tess Cottage, is **St John's Well**, supposedly the source of the **River Frome**. The poet George Crabbe was rector of Evershot from 1783-87.

The church is the setting for the last scene in *The Woodlanders* where Marty South is a solitary loyal figure at Giles Winterborne's grave. The churchyard also inspired the poem *Her Late Husband* (King's Hintock 182–), which is a reflection of Hardy's, for then, unorthodox views on marriage.

MELBURY HOUSE/KING'S-HINTOCK COURT

Mrs Charmond's house in *The Woodlanders* is not modelled on **Melbury House** but Hardy used its situation in the park and surrounding woodland. The house, however, is the **King's Hintock Court** of the first story in A *Group of Noble Dames* – the first Countess of Wessex, in which

> *King's-Hintock Court is, as we know, one of the most imposing of the mansions that overlook our beautiful Blackmoor or Blakemore Vale.*

Squire and Mrs Dornell are at loggerheads over the marriage plans for their daughter, Betty. The Squire returns to their home after a disagreement from the direction of Ivell (Yeovil):

> *he entered the mile-long drive through the park to the Court. The drive being open, without an avenue, the Squire could discern the north front and door of the Court a long way of …*

This is easily recognisable as the estate road from Clammer's Gate. The Squire's man, Tupcombe, approaches the same way at night:

> *he turned in at the lodge-gate nearest to Ivell and King's Hintock village, and pursued the long north drive – itself much like a turnpike road … Though there were so many trees in King's Hintock park, few bordered the carriage roadway; he could see it stretching ahead in the pale night light like an unrolled deal shaving. Presently the irregular frontage of the house came in view, of great extent, but low, except where it rose into the outlines of a broad square tower.*

In this story there is also a reference to the tiny church nearby, *their own little church in the shrubbery.*

The *obscure gate* to the east of King's-Hintock Park, by which Betty rode off with Charles Phelipson, still exists nearly opposite Bubb Down hill. It is not a public right of way.

The ancient stone pillar, Cross-and-Hand, stands in isolation on Batcombe Hill. Hardy describes it as *something sinister; or solemn, according to mood, in the scene amid which it stands.* Drawing: Douglas Snowdon

Melbury Park, six hundred acres covered with oaks, chestnuts and limes, with five lakes and a deer park. The Lion Gate leads into Evershot; the lions were erected in the late seventeenth century. Photographs: Rodney Legg

The main street in Evershot. the thatched cottage on the left is known as Tess Cottage. The River Frome rises at St John's Well behind the church. Drawing: Douglas Snowden.

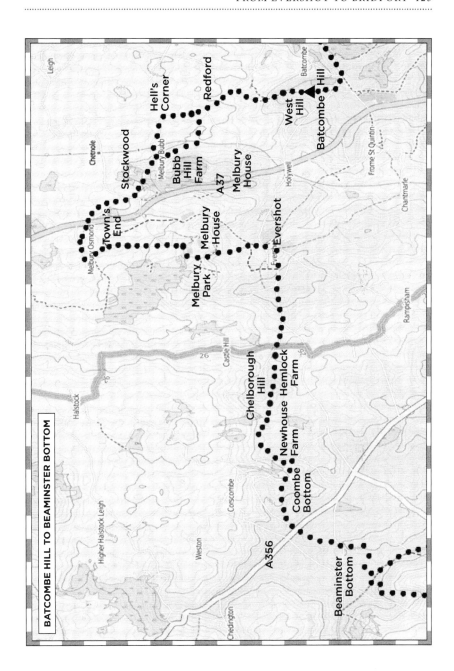

BATCOMBE HILL TO BEAMINSTER BOTTOM

EVERSHOT/EVERSHEAD

On both her outward and return journeys to Emminster Tess stopped for refreshment at the cottage west of the church – now named after her. She avoided the **Sow and Acorn (the Acorn)**. While she drinks milk at the cottage in the afternoon, the old woman who serves her describes how all the villagers have gone to hear a 'ranter' preach … *'an excellent, fiery, Christian man'*. Tess is amazed to find Alec d'Urberville addressing the crowd in a nearby barn. This was in **Tanyard**, a lane near the church; it has now been demolished.

The Sow and Acorn at **Evershead** is where Squire Dornell's man sat in the chimney corner hoping to hear news of the young Betty, who had been recently married to Stephen Reynard against her father's wishes.

The inn is also mentioned in *Interlopers at the Knap*. Philip Hall returns destitute from Australia and on his way to King's-Hintock calls in at the Sow and Acorn to see an old friend.

BENVILLE LANE/BENVILL LANE

On Chelborough Hill the route runs parallel with **Benvill Lane** to the south by which Tess travels on her way to Emminster. The lane traverses *more gentle country* than the first part of her journey. When Angel covers the same ground he scarcely notices the *hedges and trees purple with buds* that line the lane.

TOLLER DOWN

In the opening chapters of *Far from the Madding Crowd* Gabriel Oak's farm is on **Norcombe Hill** *not far from lonely* **Toller-Down**. It is

a featureless convexity of chalk and soil – … covered on its northern side by an ancient and decaying plantation of beeches, whose upper verge formed a line over the crest, fringing its arched curve against the sky, like a mane … these trees sheltered the southern slope from the keenest blasts, which smote the wood and floundered through it with a sound as of grumbling, or gushed over its crowning boughs in a weakened moan. The dry leaves in the ditch simmered and boiled in the same breezes, a tongue of air occasionally ferreting out a few, and sending them spinning across the grass …

To persons standing alone on a hill during a clear midnight such as this, the roll of the world eastward is almost a palpable movement.

FROM EVERSHOT TO BRIDPORT

From **Evershot** continue westwards on road for about a mile where turn right towards Chelborough. At the T-junction turn right then immediately left down No Through Road. Follow for a quarter of a mile to Hemlock Farm. Over the brow of hill take bridleway left off farm track up side of hill through wood into field. Follow path uphill to gate near edge of wood on right. Where the wood curves right keep straight on across **Chelborough Hill** through several gates to barns. Ignore bridleway sign to left. There is a good view of Castle Hill behind to the right beyond the village of West Chelborough. This was the site of two small medieval castles. The wooded country of Melbury Park can be seen in the background.

Pass right of barns straight ahead through gate then further gate to grassy fern-lined track ahead. After a quarter of a mile at T- junction turn left onto stony track to Newhouse Farm. Turn left on lane, pass bungalow and watch carefully for footpath sign through hedge on right. Bear right past bungalow to go through gate in hedge some way down, from where bear right down field to gap between woods to gate and cottage. Go straight ahead on bridleway up hill behind isolated cottage to follow edge of wood on left to top of field where bridlegate leads into an outstanding dry valley. Climb steadily to the right up long slope to bridlegate in hedge to continue on left diagonal across field to further bridlegate.

This is the rolling hill country of West Dorset with the tall masts of the radio station at Rampisham presiding over a landscape alternately wild and intimate, with its bleak hilltops and sheltered valleys. Left is dramatic Toller Down, 800 feet above sea level.

The A356 runs along the ridge at Toller Gate, an old turnpike, northwest through Wynyard's Gap down to Crewkerne, and south east to Dorchester. Toller Gate was once called Catsley Down Gate where, in Fair Field, a sheep fair was held.

The description is not of a specific spot but conveys a general impression of the bleakness and immensity of **Toller Down**. It is compatible with the tragedy that befalls Gabriel's sheep one **still moist night** when they are driven by his rogue dog through a hedge to plunge to their deaths in a chalk pit.

The poem *The Homecoming* is about a young bride's disillusionment with her new husband's home on *haunted Toller Down*. Hardy uses a refrain to evoke the wild and isolated nature of the place.

> *Gruffly growled the wind on Toller downland broad and bare,*
> *And lonesome was the house, and dark; and few came there.*

> *'I didn't think such furniture as this was all you'd own,*
> *And great black beams for ceiling, and a floor o'wretched stone,*
> *And nasty pewter platters, horrid forks of steel and bone,*
> *And a monstrous crock in chimney. 'Twas to me quite unbeknown!'*

> *Straight from Whit'sheet Hill to Benvill Lane the blusters pass,*
> *Hitting hedges, milestones, handposts, trees and tufts of grass.*

> *'Well, had I only known, my dear, that this was how you'd be,*
> *I'd have married her of riper years that was so fond of me.*
> *But since I can't, I've half a mind to run away to sea,*
> *And leave 'ee to go barefoot to your d—d dadee!'*

> *Gruffly growled the wind on Toller Down, so bleak and bare,*
> *And lonesome was the house and dark; and few came there.*

In another poem *The Dark-Eyed Gentleman* Hardy calls the road over Toller Down **Crimmercrock Lane**, the scene of a seduction.

WHITESHEET HILL

This features in the nostalgic *Molly Gone*, which is a remembrance of Hardy's sister, Mary, with whom he had a very close relationship.

> *No more jauntings by Molly and me*
> *To the town by the sea,*
> *Or along over Whitesheet to Wynyard's green Gap,*
> *Catching Montacute Crest*
> *To the right against Sedgmoor, and Lorton-Hill's far-distant cap,*
> *And Pilsdon and Lewsdon to west.*

Beaminster is situated in a rich agricultural district. Fires in the
seventeenth and eighteenth centuries consumed most of the town;
consequently there are few really old houses. Drawing: Douglas
Snowdon

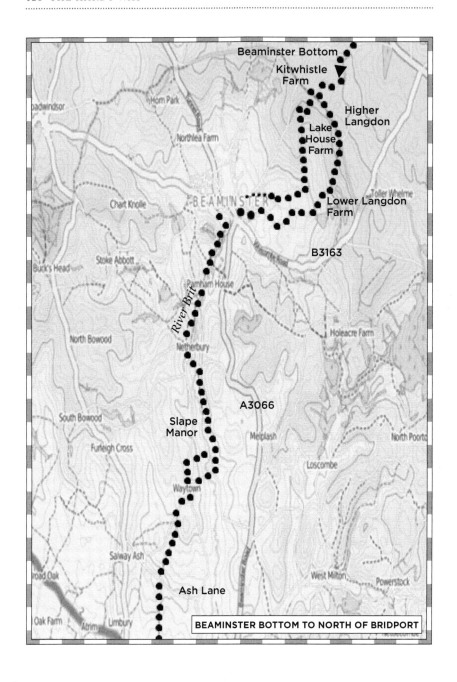

BEAMINSTER BOTTOM TO NORTH OF BRIDPORT

Turn left on minor road to cross main road onto track. Go straight ahead on bridleway to muddy exit on lane at Beaminster Bottom. Turn right then left down track just before Kitwhistle Farm. Follow the track to the end in bottom of dip in large field. Turn right through gate on bridleway then sharp left up field to bridlegate in top left hand corner. Turn right uphill to follow hedge to further bridlegate in top right hand corner of field. In next field turn right then soon left to follow edge of field to gate in top right hand corner. You are now on the **Wessex Ridgeway** again. If underfoot conditions permit you can descend most of the way into Beaminster on footpaths. If muddy there is an alternative.

Firstly the footpath option. Turn right along the Ridgeway following the sign to Beaminster. After a few yards cross stile on left into large hillside field. Walk straight on down to gate in hedge. Turn right along surfaced farm track then fork right to take track above Lake House Farm. Soon descend to cross lower track to take path into field. Follow fence to gate in bottom left hand corner of field. Enter wooded area onto rather overgrown path which fortunately soon joins a better wider one. Turn right with lakes on left. Next go through gate into field and straight on to next gate into area of mixed woodland with lake on slightly higher level to right. Leave wood over footbridge into field where turn right to follow hedge up small slope then bear right with hedge to stile in corner of field. The path is clear through a wood to footbridges over the River Brit. If not too muddy bear left over the final bridge to join path which leads to lane into **Beaminster**. Alternatively bear right up to a housing estate and then left into the town.

The wet weather route is to turn left on the Wessex Ridgeway towards Toller Whelme. Where the lane from Higher Langdon joins the route from left take path on right to a track to Langdon Manor farm then a lane to Lower Langdon Farm and town.

The sheltered small town of **Beaminster** is built in local golden orange limestone. It remains remarkably self-sufficient in that it has a variety of small, thriving local shops with attractive facades scattered round the square, with a stone roofed market cross.

One of Beaminster's most famous sons was Thomas Hine born in 1775. As a young man he went to the Cognac area of France, where he married the

BEAMINSTER/EMMINSTER

In *Tess* **Emminster Vicarage** is the home of the Reverend and Mrs Clare, Angel's parents. It is on the corner of a lane down to **St Mary's Church** from the main road. When Angel visits his parents to tell them about Tess he comes to the *hill-surrounded little town, the Tudor church-tower of red stone, the clump of trees near the vicarage* … To him this is home: to Tess, on her desperate journey more than a sad year later, it is the unknown – the sum of all her hopes, the glimmer of light at the end of a long dark tunnel. But as soon as she comes within sight of the place her confidence starts to ebb:

> *about noon she paused by a gate on the edge of the basin in which Emminster and its Vicarage lay.*
> *The square tower, beneath which she knew that at that moment the Vicar and his congregation were gathered, had a severe look in her eyes.*

She steels herself to continue and puts on her best boots, hiding her thick ones in a hedge.

> *The shrubs on the Vicarage lawn rustled uncomfortably in the frosty breeze; …*
> *The wind was so nipping that the ivy-leaves had become wizened and gray, each tapping incessantly upon its neighbour with a disquieting stir of her nerves.*

Once again circumstances defeat Tess; she leaves **Emminster** without seeing Angel's parents to face the heavy road back to Flintcomb-Ash.

NETHERBURY/CLOTON

This features in one of Hardy's less well known short stories, *Destiny and a Blue Cloak*. The mill, with its garden, orchard and paddock, bounded by a stream (the **River Brit**), is the home of Agatha. The *little wooden bridge* does not exist, but there is a stone bridge which leads over to the church.

WAYTOWN

Around **Waytown** there are a number of cider-apple orchards. Hardy wrote about the cidermaker in several of his novels and counted sweet cyder as one of the *great things* of life:

> *Sweet Cyder is a great thing,*
> *A great thing to me,*
> *Spinning down to Weymouth town*

daughter of a cognac merchant and founded the 'connoisseurs' brandy well-known today.

In the past Beaminster was a centre for rope and sail production, embroidered buttons, shoes, wrought iron work and paper and clock making. Today it is a market town and a good centre for tourism in an area of outstanding natural beauty.

The **Church of St Mary**, tucked away south of the town centre, has a pinnacled tower from the early sixteenth century that survived the Reformation, one of the finest ornamented towers in the country. On the edge of the churchyard is a former almshouse, endowed in 1630. Nearby a plaque commemorates the Great Plague when people met under a sycamore tree, holding posies to ward off the infection.

Near the church is **St Mary Well Street**, lined with mellow stone cottages. At bridge take concrete path alongside cottages to the A3066. Turn right for a few yards to path on the right over the **River Brit**. Turn left to follow river. The path soon leads up across field to two gates right of cottage. Exit through left hand gate to veer diagonally right to join the clearly defined Jubilee Trail from the deer park on left. Go through gate to continue on track parallel with **Parnham House** on left. Sixteenth century Parnham in its beautiful gardens has been splendidly restored from the original, partly by John Nash in the early nineteenth century. It was the home of John Makepeace's furniture workshops, where craftsmen used long neglected English hardwoods such as holly, mulberry and burr oak to make furniture in modern designs. **Parnham** is now a family home — the gardens rarely open to the public except on the annual occasion of the Dorset Food Fair in October. On a hill above the house is the grave of William Rhodes Moorhouse, the first airman to win the Victoria Cross. His son is also buried here, honoured for service in the Second World War.

The Jubilee Trail forks to the right but follow the main path keeping straight ahead parallel with the river until a concrete farmers' bridge on right where cross then immediately go left. Soon at fork keep left of churchyard. Ignore steps to left at first entrance to church. At main entrance turn left down steps, then left again into Netherbury. **Netherbury Church**, mostly late medieval, was restored in the nineteenth century with protected stained

By Ridgway thirstily,
And maid and mistress summoning
Who tend the hostelry:
O cyder is a great thing,
A great thing to me!

BRIDPORT/PORT BREDY

Subsequent to her parting from Angel, Tess works for a time on a dairy farm near **Port Bredy**.

The town figures in some detail in the story *Fellow Townsmen in Wessex Tales*. This begins with a wonderful description of its situation when it was obviously much smaller than it is today:

The shepherd on the east hill could shout out lambing intelligence to the shepherd on the west hill, over the intervening town chimneys, without great inconvenience to his voice, so nearly did the steep pastures encroach upon the burghers' backyards. And at night it was possible to stand in the very midst of the town and hear from their native paddocks on the lower levels of the greensward the mild lowing of the farmer's heifers, and the profound, warm blowings of breath in which those creatures indulge. But the community which had jammed itself in the valley thus flanked formed a veritable town, with a real mayor and corporation, and a staple manufacture.

The staple manufacture is of course, rope-making.

At the outset of the story, Barnet and Downe, the *fellow-burgesses* and good friends, drove into the town one damp evening:

The street was unusually still for the hour of seven in the evening; an increasing drizzle from the sea had prevailed since the afternoon, and now formed a gauze across the yellow lamps, and trickled with a gentle rattle down the heavy roofs of stone tile, that bent the house-ridges hollow-backed with its weight, and in some instances caused the walls to bulge outwards in the upper story. Their route took them past the little town-hall, the Black Bull Hotel, and onward to the junction of a small street on the right, consisting of a row of those two-and-two windowed brick residences of no particular age, which are exactly alike wherever found, except in the people they contain.

This description fits East Street, the Bull Hotel and King Street, past the Town Hall on the right going east, which was where Downe lived. Barnet

glass windows. It contains brasses of the famous local seafaring Hood family from the eighteenth century.

A hundred and fifty years ago this village, the centre of a cider-making and flax-growing area, had a population of over two thousand. Today it is tranquil with many attractive cottages but not much activity! On the left is a private house which still betrays the fact that it was once The Star Inn. Down towards the river the former mill can be seen to the left. To view turn left over bridge. The route goes to the right on a bridleway, with river on right until a weir, where bear left up field with fence on right. Pass a dew pond before going through gate behind Oxbridge cottages. Where surface becomes fully concrete turn right at cottage garage to bend sharply back on descent left to footbridge over river. Continue through new Slape Manor housing development up left to lane into **Waytown** where there is refreshment at **The Hare and Hounds**.

Leave the village along the street southwards then first right towards Salway Ash. Join a bridleway to the left opposite a barn at the end of a large cider apple orchard on left.

The next couple of miles are over mixed farming country, mainly dairy and arable. Pass between banks and through a bridlegate to right of farm gate with wind farm ahead to go straight ahead to the right of cottages. Go down a stretch of grass past cottages and follow the bridleway straight ahead down field with hedge on left. Keep straight on down, cross stream and then uphill to Ash Lane. Turn left then first right on track leading to Higher Ash Farm. Continue on bridleway down fields to a dip and then up always on bridleway to another lane. Here there is an option to follow a footpath straight over field to **Middle Pymore Farm** or to turn left on lane and then immediately right down farm lane to the same point. When I passed one August day there was a gathering of mainly middle-aged men flying remote control planes. The farm is walker friendly and there is a clearly marked footpath which passes to the right of the farm buildings to lead down fields with hedge on left. In dip cross stream and then on until path joins road at Court Orchard housing estate at **Allington**, north west of **Bridport**. Very soon turn right to join the B3162 southwards to town centre.

The warehouses of the Bridport Brewery line the River Brit. The brewery was established in 1794 and the main office building on the other side is thatched. Photograph: Rodney Legg

The name **Bridport** is synonymous with rope making, which has taken place here for over 750 years. The town is internationally known as a centre of production for fishing nets, lines, twines and cordage. Wimbledon tennis nets are amongst its products, with artificial fibres having for the most part replaced traditional hemp or flax. A museum in **South Street** details this important industry. The whole atmosphere of the town is permeated with evidence of rope-making; the many broad pavements or 'walks' are where the new rope was laid out to dry when the industry was cottage-based. Later production moved to the mills and these can be seen in the back streets and along the edge of the River Brit, where flax was once grown. Perhaps a measure of the industry's fame is the saying 'to be stabbed by a Bridport dagger', which means to be hanged!

Bridport is an ancient market town mentioned in Doomsday, when it had a mint and an ecclesiastical establishment. On the eastern outskirts there is a stone monument which commemorates the escape of Charles II, fleeing after the Battle of Worcester with a price of £1,000 on his head. He evaded the Cromwellians by diverting to a hiding place from **Lee Lane**, where the stone stands.

In 1857 Bridport was linked to the Dorchester railway line via Maiden Newton, but like so many lines, this was lost in 1975.

The Georgian town hall and market house, with distinctive clock tower, protrude into the road on the corner of East and South Streets. The latter is particularly attractive with its eighteenth and nineteenth century houses and some of earlier date, including **The Chantry,** a very unusual medieval building with modern windows.

There are many churches and chapels in Bridport. The Wesleyan Methodist Chapel in South Street dates from 1838 but is now an Arts Centre; the Congregational Church (1860) is in East Street as also are the United Reform Church (1859), with porches on both sides, and a Unitarian chapel of 1794. The parish church of St Mary, on the west side of South Street, dates from the fourteenth century and was restored in the 1860s by John Hicks of Dorchester, with whom Hardy trained as an architect when he left school. It has an impressive pulpit in Caen stone.

lived in East Street, *the main street,* where his house was later *bought by the trustees of the Congregational Baptist body* and pulled down to enable the building of a new chapel.

The road to **West Bay** is today lined with houses and bungalows. When Barnet went to call on Lucy Saville it was quite rural. Lucy's cottage was at the West Bay end, possibly No 74. **Chateau Ringdale,** the more pretentious mansion that Mrs Barnet was so anxious to acquire, was also on the West Bay road; the site exists but not the house. It is in a road to the left going towards West Bay called **Wanderwell**.

Barnet often walked

the lower lanes of the borough, where the rope-walks stretched in which his family formerly had share, and looked at the rope-makers walking backwards, overhung by apple-trees and bushes, and intruded on by cows and calves, as if trade had established itself there at considerable inconvenience to Nature.

Until the end of the last century, 'yarn' was twisted into 'strands' which were twisted into ropes by men who put the strands round their waists, secured the free ends to a hook and walked backwards away from the hook on rope-walks, paying out and twisting the yarn into rope.

The marriage of Downe and Lucy takes place in **St Mary's Church**.

Nearby is **The Five Bells**, likely to be *The Ring of Bells* in *The Whaler's Wife*, a narrative poem of tragedy through misunderstanding.

WEST BAY

The sea at **West Bay** can be very fierce and unpredictable, as it was on the day Mrs Downe and Mrs Barnet were capsized in their boat in *Fellow Townsmen.* On that day Barnet walked down to the sea from Bridport:

As he went a sudden blast of air came over the hill … and spoilt the previous quiet of the scene. The wind had already shifted violently, and now smelt of the sea.

The harbour-road soon began to justify its name. A gap appeared in the rampart of hills which shut out the sea, and on the left of the opening rose a vertical cliff, coloured a burning orange by the sunlight, the companion cliff on the right being livid in shade. Between these cliffs, like the Libyan bay which sheltered the shipwrecked Trojans, was a little haven, seemingly a beginning

On the other side of the road, a short way south, are the almshouses and courtyard of the Friends' Meeting House. The almshouses were fifteenth and sixteenth century town houses; the Quakers, illegal in their early days in the seventeenth century, met in the adjoining barn.

A rough sea off West Bay, formerly Bridport Harbour. It was re-named by the Great Western Railway in 1884, when hopes were high that the port would become a holiday resort. Engraving: J.M.W. Turner

The Hardy Way looking towards Portland from The Fleet. Photograph by Arthur Simmonds.

made by Nature herself of a perfect harbour, which appealed to the passer-by as only requiring a little human industry to finish it and make it famous, the ground on each side as far back as the daisied slopes that bounded the interior valley being a mere layer of blown sand.

Hardy neatly sums up the problem of the silting up of the harbour:

But the Port-Bredy burgesses a mile inland had, in the course of ten centuries, responded to that mute appeal with the result that the tides had invariably choked up their works with sand and shingle as soon as completed.

The first part of *Fellow Townsmen* takes place in the mid 1840s when West Bay was very small:

There were but few houses here: a rough pier, a few boats, some stores, an inn, a residence or two, a ketch unloading in the harbour, were the chief features of the settlement.

Twenty-one years later, when George Barnet returns, the railway has *invaded* Port Bredy, but not yet West Bay, which is little changed.

The **Harbour Inn** mentioned in the story is the **Bridport Arms Hotel**, which is mostly stone and thatch and dates from the seventeenth century.

CHESIL BEACH/PEBBLE BEACH

In *The Well-Beloved*, his last novel, set for the most part on the Isle of Slingers (Portland) Hardy refers to Chesil as **Pebble Beach**; he is here concerned mainly with the Portland end of the bank.

West Bay station in 1910. A G.W.R. mixed train on the morning service. The station's canopy is a classic of the period. Source: Rodney Legg collection

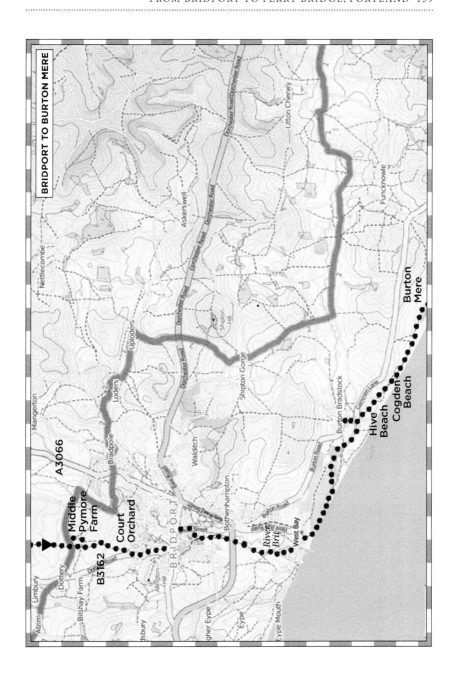

At 784 feet up on Blackdown Hill, the octagonal stone monument to Nelson's Hardy stands 70 feet high with panoramic views. It was erected in 1844-46. Photograph: Colin Graham

FROM BRIDPORT TO FERRY BRIDGE, PORTLAND

Leave Bridport behind St Mary's on a path to a bridge across the River Brit. Cross, turn left to follow river past the rear of warehouses and a brewery with fine old water wheel. Soon the well-defined path to **West Bay** veers away from the river to pass beneath the A35T and cross several flat meadows once used for growing flax but now grazed by sheep. At a static caravan park bear left through caravans to emerge on the harbour at West Bay.

In 1884, in the hope that West Bay would become a holiday resort, the railway was extended to a terminus in the village (the station can still be seen behind the beach). Now, many years later, the little fishing port is also a busy tourist spot and marina. There is an amazing fish restaurant, The Riverside.

The harbour was created in 1744. To prevent continual silting up by shingle from Chesil Beach, the River Brit is dammed with sluices under the road bridge. When the valley becomes full of water the river is released to surge through and clear the harbour. The west side is protected by lumps of Portland stone and concrete blocks. For a hundred and fifty years shipbuilding flourished here but declined with the advent of iron boats; the last launching being in 1879. There was also a good timber trade with Scandinavia.

Leave by the steep **East Cliff** of vertical sandstone on the South West Coast Path across springy turf with fine views west to Golden Cap and Lyme Regis. Serious cliff erosion in the area was exacerbated by the storms in February 2014. Keep well away from the cliff edge. At end of golf course, Dorset's first (1891), continue on Coast Path down and then along Burton Freshwater keeping a huge caravan/mobile home site on left until it becomes necessary to go through it for a short way. Keep as close as possible to seaward edge to re-emerge to a bridge over the River Bride where cross and leave the Coast Path to turn left through a field parallel with river into **Burton Bradstock**, a pretty village with many seventeenth

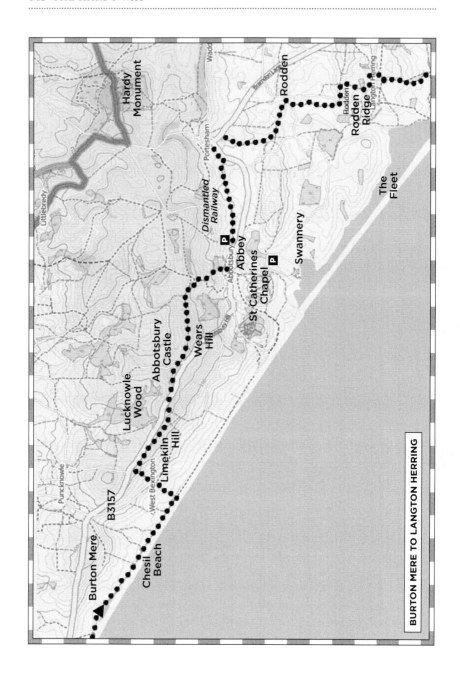

and eighteenth century cottages in local golden stone. Once a busy fishing village with fourteen pubs it is now mainly concerned with tourism. It also had a flax mill for ropes and nets which still stands in **Mill Street**, near the medieval church.

Return to the coast path by a footpath left from Cliff Road signposted Burton Beach. Follow across National Trust land diagonally over a large field, through kissing gate and across the next field. Head down towards the car park at **Hive Beach**. In the winter of 1943-4 soldiers practised on **Burton Beach** for the invasion of Normandy. Rejoin the Coast Path to pass the Old Coastguard caravan site to **Cogden Beach**, part of **Chesil Beach**, a huge shingle bank which extends for eighteen miles from Bridport to Portland. It becomes more pronounced from just east of Burton at Burton Mere and even more so from Abbotsbury eastwards where it cuts off a long lagoon of partly salt, partly fresh water, **The Fleet**, which was once used by smugglers to sink their contraband until it could be safely retrieved. At the Portland end the Bank is nearly two hundred yards wide and about fifty feet high, a dangerous part of the coast in bad weather, responsible for many shipwrecks. In the 1820s a five hundred ton ship was blown right over the bank. There is a severe undertow as the sea rushes back over the pebbles making swimming extremely hazardous. As if to compensate, the flora and bird life are rich and unusual: plants that thrive on the shingle include blue sea-kale, sea pea, white campion and yellow horned sea poppies with curling green seed pods. Birds include winter wildfowl, herons and reed and sedge warblers. The name 'Chesil' derives from an Anglo-Saxon word meaning pebble. A peculiarity of the Bank is that the pebbles get larger from west to east, a phenomenon unknown elsewhere.

Follow the path for a short way along Cogden Beach then turn inland behind **Burton Mere** where the walking is easier. In wet conditions it may be necessary to go back onto the beach sooner but otherwise follow the path until about half a mile from **West Bexington** where it goes back on the beach. **Chesil Beach** is wild and unique; on a fine day the sun glistens on the meres while sea and marsh birds wheel and cry; in stormy weather the sea is magnificent as it crashes against the shingle. Just before arriving at West Bexington there is a large reed bed, wet meadows and scrub, which are a nature reserve of the Dorset Wildlife Trust.

ABBOTSBURY/ABBOTSEA/ABBOT BEACH

Perhaps surprisingly **Abbotsbury** is mentioned only in passing in Hardy's work.

PORTESHAM/POS'HAM

In *The Trumpet Major* Bob Loveday visits Captain Hardy at **Pos'ham** to ask if he can serve on the *Victory*. He walks across from Overcombe (Sutton Poyntz) to *the small manor-house at Pos'ham* a few miles away where Captain Hardy *usually spent the intervals between his different cruises.*

> *By the time that he reached the village it was dark, and the larger stars had begun to shine when he walked up to the door of the old-fashioned house which was the family residence of this branch of the South-Wessex Hardys ...*

> *The captain at this time was a bachelor of thirty-five, rather stout in build, with light eyes, bushy eyebrows, a square broad face, plenty of chin, and a mouth whose corners played between humour and grimness.*

He agrees to 'ask' for Bob and gives him a *glass of grog* to sustain him on his walk back to Overcombe Mill.

BLACKDOWN HILL/BLACK'ON

Nearly the whole population of Overcombe climb to the Ridgeway to see King George III review his troops on the downs:

> *It was a clear day with little wind stirring, and the view from the downs, one of the most extensive in the county, was unclouded. The eye of any observer who cared for such things swept over the wave-washed town, and the bay beyond, and the Isle, with its pebble bank, lying on the sea to the left of these, like a great crouching animal tethered to the mainland.*

To the west Black'on could be seen,

> *the beacon thereon being built of furze faggots thatched with straw, and standing on the spot where the monument now raises its head.*

The novel is set in Napoleonic times when the south of England was in a state of perpetual expectation of an invasion.

Black'on is also mentioned in the poem *After the Club-Dance*, the third poem in the group called *At Casterbridge Fair* in which Maidon is Maiden Castle,

Bexington Beach was used by smugglers in the eighteenth and early nineteenth centuries. Leave the beach to pass the car park to turn inland up a lane. Where this bears left go straight on up a track signposted to the **Hardy Monument** (the Admiral, not our Thomas!). Take a right fork with similar sign.

This brings you out on **Limekiln Hill**, named after the lime kiln nearby which has been restored by the National Trust and the Dorset Trust for Nature Conservation and which may be seen just over the edge of the slope not far from where the path emerges on the hillside. Lime was once produced here for whitewash, plaster and mortar and for use on the land. Limestone and anthracite were deposited at the top and the quicklime extracted from the bottom. Follow the path, now also the Dorset Ridgeway, with the contours of the hill on the seaward side of the meadow, parallel with the road, for just under a mile, past tumuli on the left and with glorious views along the coast to Portland. At the tumuli bear left towards the road until nearly level with **Abbotsbury Castle**, an Iron Age hill fort on the left. Cross a stile and the road to this.

The view in all directions is amazing and worth the climb. Continue eastwards to cross lane to **Wears Hill**, north west of Abbotsbury. The walk along the Ridgeway for about a mile is one of the finest stretches of the whole walk, high and wide and handsome. St Catherine's Chapel, on Chapel Hill south of Abbotsbury, stands out as a sea and land mark. On a fine day this ridge is a place to linger, to picnic, but it was cold on the October afternoon when I walked here so I was glad to find a sign pointing to **Abbotsbury**, where a hot cup of tea and scones made me very happy.

The Benedictine Abbey from which the village takes its name already existed at the time of the Norman invasion and is recorded in Doomsday. Like many other such monasteries it perished at the Reformation so that only ruins of the monastic complex remain. Thankfully the fifteenth century 275 feet long tithe barn was spared. In use until recently it now houses a collection of rural bygones. It is thatched with reeds cut from the Fleet. Walls around the later Church of St Nicholas are all that remain of the abbey. A battle in the Civil War left bullet holes in the back of the pulpit. St Catherine's Chapel, dedicated to the patron saint of spinsters, was also spared because of its use as a sea mark. Over five hundred years old it has stone roof vaulting and walls four feet thick.

the prehistoric hill fort a couple of miles south west of Dorchester. Parish clubs or friendly societies organised dances and club walking (ceremonial processions with dance). This young woman questions her feeling of shame for having flouted the sexual inhibitions imposed on her by Victorian convention.

Black'on frowns east on Maidon,
  And westward to the sea,
But on neither is his frown laden
  With scorn, as his frown on me!

At dawn my heart grew heavy,
  I could not sip the wine,
I left the jocund bevy
  And that young man o'mine.

The roadside elms pass by me, _
  Why do I sink with shame
When the birds a-perch there eye me?
  They, too, have done the same!

In the short story *A Tryst at an Ancient Earthwork* Hardy described Maiden Castle *as an enormous many-limbed organism of an antediluvian time … lying lifeless, and covered with a thin green cloth, which hides its substance, whilst revealing its contour.* Photograph: Colin Graham

Abbotsbury is a mellow village built mainly in local orange ochre limestone with many thatched cottages. The growth and manufacture of hemp for the rope industry once took place here. The **Swannery** on the shore of the Fleet was started in the fourteenth century by monks to provide food! Swans have nested here for hundreds of years and there is also a colony of terns in a nature reserve across the Fleet.

The village seems an unlikely place to find sub-tropical gardens but the Earl of Ilchester, who had a home at Abbotsbury Castle (not the hill fort!), started the gardens in a sheltered frost free valley south west of the village in the early nineteenth century. The castle has gone but the gardens flourish and attract many visitors.

Leave Abbotsbury by the B3157 in the direction of Portesham and Weymouth. On the outskirts of the village a bridleway branches off left onto the track of the dismantled railway. Follow this for over a mile to **Portesham**. Nostalgic of the age of the small country railway before economics and Beeching eradicated it, this makes a tranquil contrast to the heady walk on the downs. Portesham lies at the foot of **Portesham Hill**, near **Blackdown Hill** on which stands the **Hardy Monument**. Admiral Sir Thomas Masterman Hardy lived here until 1807. His small Georgian manor, with its pillared porch and iron railings, can be seen at the corner of the main road and the minor road to Portesham Hill. The Admiral, captain of Nelson's flagship, was famously present at the great man's death at the Battle of Trafalgar in 1805. Literary Hardy, always hoping to trace illustrious forebears, believed that he was related to the Admiral and corresponded with his daughter about her father's life and ancestry.

The church of St Peter is mainly restored and medieval. On the south wall the tomb of William Weare is half inside and half outside the church. He was a Royalist who died in 1670 and requested this curious arrangement. As in Abbotsbury church there is evidence here too of the Civil War where a number of musket balls were removed from the south door.

Leave Portesham by the Weymouth road. Pass a garage then turn right into the entrance to **Portesham Dairy Farm** campsite. Do not go into site but take right-hand track alongside it to turn immediately left across footbridge into small wood then up past buildings keeping left to stile then

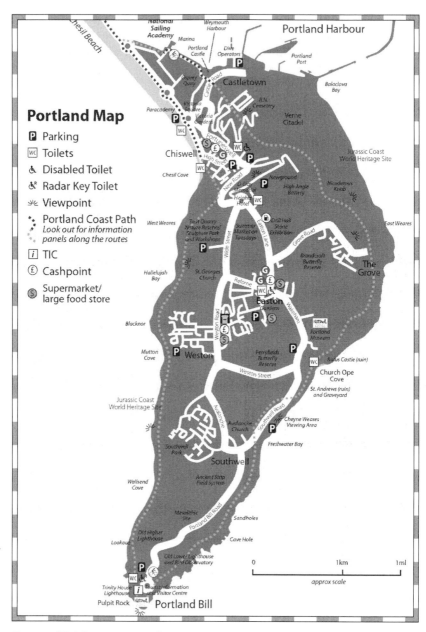

Portland Map

P Parking

WC Toilets

& Disabled Toilet

&ᴿ Radar Key Toilet

⁂ Viewpoint

•⁚ Portland Coast Path
⁚ *Look out for information*
°₀ *panels along the routes*

i TIC

£ Cashpoint

S Supermarket/
  large food store

Courtesy of Visit Dorset. www.visit-dorset.com

narrow path between trees to gate on left. Continue along hedge with an excellent view of St Catherine's Chapel. At top left-hand corner of field go over stile then turn left along hedge towards farm buildings. At the end of the field go straight on down permissive path to left of farmyard at the end of which turn left to skirt house on right keeping slightly left to reach the bottom of an uphill field where ascend with hedge on left. Continue straight on to a grass ridge that separates two fields. Turn left to gate. (If the crossing to ridge is difficult follow round edge of field to the right keeping hedge then fence on left up to gate at the end of the ridge). Follow straight ahead to gate with good views all round and strip lynchets to right, then cross field with fence on right. At end through gate and continue straight on downhill to **Rodden**, where there is an attractive Georgian house.

On lane turn right for a few yards past cottages on left to turn through a gate on left and cross field keeping parallel with stream on left to crossing place a good way up long field. Over the stream cross next field straight ahead to gate in the direction of **Rodden Ridge**, heading for signpost on skyline. Climb field with hedge to turn left then right onto lane. Cross to right-hand gate to ascend field alongside hedge. Soon after stile of footpath from left turn right down field beyond hedge and wall. This is a good place for a break with stunning views north to the Hardy Monument and south to the Fleet and Chesil. Continue down hill alongside stone wall towards **Langton Herring**. A very large German Shepherd dog attached itself to us at this point which we had to re-locate in the village with some difficulty! Half way down cross into adjacent field and at bottom turn sharp left up side of hedge to stile onto lane. Turn left then second right at telephone kiosk into the village.

The Lords of the Manor here in the Middle Ages were called Herring. The church of St Peter is medieval with nineteenth restoration; its small tower is probably eighteenth century. Many of the buildings are in local yellow stone. Pass the **Elm Tree Inn** and follow straight on down to the end of Shop Lane then bend right to the entrance to Chapel Close where turn left along a track to **The Fleet**, which the path then follows until it cuts across the **Herbury** promontory to reach a large ugly conglomeration of buildings which are the **Moonfleet Hotel** and its leisure facilities. Hurriedly pass these along the coast path round the next promontory and adjacent

PORTLAND/THE ISLE OF SLINGERS/THE ISLE BY THE RACE

Prehistoric man used pebbles for slingstones and it is probable that Hardy had this in mind when he chose his name for **Portland**. It is interesting that after his death, excavations at Maiden Castle, near Dorchester, revealed thousands of pebbles from Chesil Beach that had been assembled for this purpose.

In *The Trumpet-Major* Anne Garland has to be rowed across the Fleet on her way to **Portland Bill** because no bridge existed then.

Hardy introduces the 'isle' in the preface to *The Well-Beloved* as *The peninsula carved by Time out of a single stone* and the opening lines of the novel describe it as

> *that Gibraltar of Wessex, the singular peninsula once an island, and still called such, that stretches out like the head of a bird into the English Channel.*

The causeway is a *long thin neck of pebbles* 'cast up by rages of the sea', *and unparalleled in its kind in Europe*. On his walk to Budmouth (Weymouth) one evening, Jocelyn Pierston waits in vain for Avice Caro *on the pebble ridge which walled out the sea* and here he reads her note cancelling their meeting. He continues alone as a storm brews:

> *In such an exposed spot the night wind was gusty, and the sea behind the pebble barrier kicked and flounced in complex rhythms, which could be translated equally well as shocks of battle or shouts of thanksgiving.*

He overtakes Marcia Bencomb and they shelter together under a lerret (a small fishing boat) and listen to the *canine crunching of pebbles by the sea*. Eventually they move on,

> *through the twanging and spinning storm. The sea rolled and rose so high on their left, and was so near them on their right, that it seemed as if they were traversing its bottom like the Children of Israel. Nothing but the frail bank of pebbles divided them from the raging gulf without, and at every bang of the tide against it the ground shook, the shingle clashed, the spray rose vertically, and was blown over their heads. Quantities of sea-water trickled through the pebble wall, and ran in rivulets across their path to join the sea within. The 'Island' was an island still.*

Later, when Pierston returns to his island home as a young man of forty, he finds that a railway has been constructed:

to a horse-training all weather gallop and so to **East Fleet**, a tiny hamlet with the remnants of an old grey church wrecked by a great storm in 1824, when the sea broke through Chesil Bank. This event featured in J. Meade Falkner's novel, *Moonfleet*, when the vault of the church was used by smugglers to store their great casks of brandy. There are brasses to the Mohun family whose coffins shared the vaults with brandy in the story.

East Fleet is also the name given to the eastern part of the Fleet, where the scientist Barnes Wallis tested his bouncing bomb which was responsible for the destruction of the Mohne Dam in Germany during the Second World War.

Leave the coastal path for a while to turn inland for a short way before turning right just past the church through a gate and field to join two lanes. Follow the small one eastwards through East Fleet Farm and campsite to a sharp left-hand bend. Go through a gate on the right and cross several fields then through Chickerell Camp army rifle range, where a sentry will be on duty if shooting is scheduled. Usually though carry straight on across the range to aim for another sentry box and flag post near a stile. At the end of the rifle range turn right to rejoin the coastal path at **Tidmoor Cove**.

At this point the Fleet becomes very narrow. Follow the coastal path to the Royal Engineers Bridging Camp where divert inland around the perimeter. On the east side the path returns to the Fleet for the next one-and-a-quarter miles when it reaches **Ferry Bridge** and the causeway to **Portland**.

West Weares, near Tout Quarry, Isle of Portland. A magnificently rugged stretch of coast looking north west towards Chesil Bank. The Hardy Way passes through intimidating stone bastions once the scene of working quarries. Photograph by Arthur Simmonds.

along the pebble bank, so that, except where the rails were washed away by the tides, which was rather often, the peninsula was quickly accessible. At two o'clock in the afternoon he was rattled along by this new means of locomotion, under the familiar monotonous line of bran-coloured stones, and he soon emerged from the station, which stood as a strange exotic among the black lerrets, the ruins of the washed-away village, and the white cubes of oolite, just come in view after burial through unreckonable geologic years.

The 'washed-away village' refers to **Chiswell** after the 1824 storm.

When Pierston returns twenty years later he passes over

the long featureless rib of grinding pebbles that screened off the outer sea, which could be heard lifting and dipping rhythmically in the wide vagueness of the Bay.

FORTUNESWELL/STREET OF WELLS

When Anne Garland climbs Portland Hill she finds that:

The steep incline before her was dotted with houses, showing the pleasant peculiarity of one man's doorstep being behind his neighbour's chimney, and slabs of stone as the common material for walls, roof, floor, pig-sty, stable-manger, door-scraper, and garden-stile.

The description in *The Well-Beloved* when Jocelyn climbs the same route as a young man is similar but more detailed:

The towering rock, the houses above houses, one man's doorstep rising behind his neighbour's chimney, the gardens hung up by one edge to the sky, the vegetables growing on apparently almost vertical planes, the unity of the whole island as a solid and single block of limestone four miles long, were no longer familiar and commonplace ideas. All now stood dazzlingly unique and white against the tinted sea, and the sun flashed on infinitely stratified walls of oolite.
The melancholy ruins
Of cancelled cycles, …
with a distinctiveness that called the eyes to it as strongly as any spectacle he had beheld afar.

He has been away for nearly four years and has forgotten the unique character of the place. As he traverses the plateau the sounds of quarrying greet him:

Church Ope Cove on the east side of the Isle of Portland with Rufus Castle in the background. the East Weares, a wide tract of undercliff strewn with boulders amid which grow turf, wild flowers, ferns and brambles, extend for more than a mile from Church Ope. Drawing: Douglas Snowdon

The two mile incline-operated Merchants' Railway in 1920 nearly a hundred years after its construction. Originally a charge of eight pence per mile was made for a ton of stone. Source: Rodney Legg collection

Rufus or Bow and Arrow Castle from the north side. The main business of Portland –quarrying – is everywhere evident. Pennsylvania Castle is in the background. Engraving: J.M.W. Turner

PORTLAND

The so-called **Isle of Portland** is not in fact an island as it is joined to the mainland by Chesil Bank. In effect however, it looks and feels like one because it has a unique character perhaps due to its stony heart; it is a gigantic mass of limestone some four miles long by just over one-and-a-half miles wide at its widest part.

At the north end of the causeway is **Small Mouth**, the only entrance into the Fleet. Until 1839 this had to be crossed by ferry to the island but after the Great Gale in 1824, in which the ferry was destroyed, a bridge was built. The first timber structure lasted until the 1890s. The present one dates from the 1980s. Wooden viaducts across **Weymouth Backwater** and the Fleet brought the railway to Portland in the 1860s. The iron replacements for these were demolished following the closure of the line in 1965.

Follow the A353 across the causeway. It is refreshing to report that walking conditions on Portland are excellent once you leave the heavily built-up area known as **Underhill**. The islanders pride themselves on their traditional rights of way and the whole island is criss-crossed with footpaths, although no bridleways, making a clearly defined route hardly necessary. The Hardy Way follows the route of the Portland Coast Path most of the way as shown on the map with occasional diversions as described in the text.

The harbour was sold by the Royal Navy in 1996. Portland Port is now a commercial port with a wide variety of activities including water sports and is a service station for Channel shipping.

At the first mini roundabout take the first exit along Hamm Beach Road to pass the Weymouth and Portland Sailing Academy on **Osprey Quay**, which hosted the sailing events in the 2012 Olympics. At the next roundabout continue left of the Portland Marina, where there is a good restaurant, the Harbour Lights, open every day from breakfast through to dinner (on most evenings). Follow the red brick walkway on the harbour side of buildings. There is a poignant monument to 29 young men, the youngest 17 and most under 20, who perished in the Liberty boat when attempting rescue of the

whirr-whirr, saw-saw-saw. Those were the island's snores – the noises of the quarrymen and stone-sawyers.

He becomes absorbed by the once familiar scenes of industry:

Jocelyn ... glanced across the common at the great yards within which eternal saws were going to and fro upon eternal blocks of stone – the very same saws and the very same blocks that he had seen there when last in the island, so it seemed to him ...

The timelessness of the island quarrying is apparent when Jocelyn returns as a man of sixty:

the hoary peninsula called an island looked just the same as before; ... The silent ships came and went from the wharf, the chisels clinked in the quarries; file after file of whitey-brown horses, in strings of eight or ten, painfully dragged down the hill the square blocks of stone on the antediluvian wooden wheels just as usual.

At Top-o'-Hill – as the summit of the rock was mostly called – he stood looking at the busy doings in the quarries beyond, where the numerous black hoisting-cranes scattered over the central plateau had the appearance of a swarm of crane-flies resting there.

EASTON/EAST QUARRIERS (INCLUDING WAKEHAM)

Avice Caro's home is described as:

a roomy cottage or homestead. Like the island it was all of stone, not only in walls but in window-frames, roof, chimneys, fence, stile, pigsty and stable, almost door.

This multiplicity of *quaint and massive stone features* made the cottage *capable even now of longer resistance to the rasp of Time* than ordinary new erections. The fence, stile, pigsty and stable do not exist but the stony essence of the cottage remains the same.

PENNSYLVANIA CASTLE/SYLVANIA CASTLE

Marcia Bencomb rented this prior to her meeting with Jocelyn. Twenty years later Jocelyn also rents it in order to be near the second Avice. Hardy describes it as:

a private mansion of comparatively modern date, in whose grounds stood the single plantation of trees of which the isle could boast ... a dignified manor-house in a nook by the cliffs, with modern castellations and battlements.

crew of aircraft carrier, HMS *Illustrious* which sank in the harbour in a gale in October 1948.

At the end of red path turn left on Coast Path along Liberty Road, **Portland Castle** to left. The castle was built by Henry VIII, together with ruined Sandsfoot Castle on the Weymouth shore, to protect the anchorage between Portland and Weymouth. Owned by English Heritage it is open to the public between April and November. At T-junction turn left along Castle Road to Castletown roundabout. On the landward side take public footpath under tunnel to a steep ascending track. An information plaque on each side of a stone pillar before the tunnel details **The Merchants' Incline**. It is the route of the old Merchants' Railway, constructed in 1826 to move stone down to the loading pier at Castletown for the construction of **Portland Harbour**. The rails were removed in 1959 but some of the stone sleepers remain. Climb through a housing estate once used by staff of the naval base. There are good views of the harbour, the Nothe Fort and Weymouth.

Before the mid-nineteenth century Portland's natural harbour was part of Weymouth Bay but it was then decided to construct three harbour breakwaters with Portland stone, a mammoth 23-year project resulting in the largest man-made harbour in the world, an important naval port in two World Wars and a submarine base. Hardy went aboard the American battleship *Connecticut* in **Portland Roads** in 1910 and later the same year he visited HMS *Dreadnought* and went to a dance on the US flagship *Louisiana*. Twelve years later he visited the *Queen Elizabeth* off Portland.

The stone used for making the breakwaters was quarried from **Verne Hill**, up ahead on the left. The enormous amount of earth and stone removed enabled the construction of a fort, known as the **Verne Citadel**, with deep stone-lined ditches and high ramparts, today a grim-looking prison. Just before the track reaches the road to the prison bear right through tunnel towards Portland Heights, with **Fortuneswell** spread out below to the right. Continue with the contours of the hill, always taking the left hand option on the Coast Path, nearest the huge mound of the prison. Climb steep flight of steps up to corner of Verne Hill Road where continue straight on and then left round bend still on Coast Path. To view the derelict fort of **High Angle Battery** soon leave the path at information point on the right

It had evergreen shrubs in front of it capable of weathering the whipping salt gales which sped past the walls.

RUFUS CASTLE/BOW-AND-ARROW CASTLE/THE RED KING'S CASTLE

Pierston visits the *castle overhanging the cliff* and sees his initials carved on the stones with those of Avice Caro.

The third Avice meets her lover, Henri Leverre, here before eloping from **Hope Cove**. The castle stands as a square black mass against the moonlit, indefinite sea.

ST ANDREW'S CHURCHYARD/HOPE CHURCHYARD

The *solemn spot* where Pierston kissed Avice Caro.

The twain wandered a long way that night … so far as to old Hope Churchyard, which lay in a ravine formed by a landslip ages ago. The church had slipped down with the rest of the cliff, and had long been a ruin. It seemed to say that in this last local stronghold of the Pagan divinities, where Pagan customs lingered yet, Christianity had established itself precariously at best.

CAVE HOLE

On their walk to the Bill Pierston and Avice Caro pause *over the treacherous cavern known as Cave Hole, into which the sea roared and splashed now as it had done when they visited it together as children.*

PORTLAND BILL/THE BILL/THE BEAL

Natives of Portland call it **The Beal**.

In *The Trumpet Major* Anne Garland Goes to the Beal to watch Bob Loveday sail past on HMS *Victory*.

The wild, herbless, weather-worn promontory was quite a solitude, and, saving the one old lighthouse about fifty yards up the slope, scarce a mark was visible to show that humanity had ever been near the spot. Anne found herself a seat on a stone, and swept with her eyes the tremulous expanse of water around her that seemed to utter a ceaseless unintelligible incantation. Out of the three hundred and sixty degrees of her complete horizon two hundred and fifty were covered by waves, the coup d'oeil including the area of troubled waters known

opposite a farmhouse. Dating from 1892 this is a strange ghostly place where you expect to hear the reverberations of artillery, but the only sound is that of quarrying getting progressively nearer. It was constructed in a derelict stone quarry as part of coastal defences of Portland Harbour to protect naval and merchant shipping – the guns hidden from the view of any enemy.

Return to path to go through a gateway towards the formidable grey building of Grove Young Offenders Institution, built in the mid-nineteenth century to house the convicts who worked to transport stone for the construction of the harbour breakwater. Two of Hardy's cousins became prison warders on Portland.

The area is littered with huge slabs of discarded stone. Here leave the coast path for a while. In sight of perimeter fence of the Grove take a grassy path off right to St Peter's Church. Sounds of activity are now very near from a quarry on right. Until the late nineteenth century quarries were confined to the cliff sides. Now they have made voracious bites all over the island as the stone is highly prized for its durable qualities. It has been used for some of the country's most famous buildings, including St Paul's Cathedral, London. When Hardy was eighty-seven he watched great blocks of Portland stone being transported on the railway past Max Gate, Dorchester, and commented that he thought the shape of Portland would eventually change.

St Peter's Church would look more at home in central France than here on often bleak Portland. Built in Romanesque style by convict labour in the 1870s, it has a huge ugly pulpit carved from a single block of stone. Continue on round to right of church then turn right in **Grove Road**. Soon take a footpath left which passes allotments. Keep on the main path bearing right to reach a children's playground. Turn right, then left again on Grove Road and so to **Easton**, one of the five ancient hamlets on Tophill. The main street is wide and handsome with many nineteenth century buildings and an elegant square.

Continue south on main road for about a half mile to **Wakeham**, where Hardy lunched at **The Mermaid Inn** at Easter 1890 and chatted with stone-masons. This has been converted to residences. On the corner of

as the Race, where two seas met to effect the destruction of such vessels as could not be mastered by one ...
The great silent ship, with her population of blue-jackets, marines, officers, captain, and the admiral who was not to return alive, passed like a phantom the meridian of the Bill. Sometimes her aspect was that of a large white bat, sometimes that of a grey one.

Anne returns to the mainland on a lerret from Hope Cove.

The third Avice and Henri Leverre take a fishing-lerret without oars from the beach of the cove. They get caught in the current which is

of a complicated kind ... called 'The Southern' by local sailors ... It caught the lovers' hapless boat in a few moments, and, unable to row across it – mere rivers width that it was – they beheld the grey rocks near them, and the grim wrinkled forehead of the isle above, sliding away northwards.

One of Hardy's finest poems, *The Souls of the Slain*, written in 1899 at the time of the Boer War, tells of the souls of men killed in Africa homing overhead at **Portland Bill**.

I
The thick lids of Night closed upon me
Alone at the Bill
Of the Isle by the Race –
Many-caverned, bald, wrinkled of face –
And with darkness and silence the spirit was on me
To brood and be still.

II
No wind fanned the flats of the ocean,
Or promontory sides,
Or the ooze by the strand,
Or the bent-bearded slope of the land,
Whose base took its rest amid everlong motion
Of criss-crossing tides.

III
Soon from out of the Southward seemed nearing
A whirr, as of wings
Waved by mighty-vanned flies,

Church Ope Road the **Portland Museum** occupies one of the few thatched cottages on Portland. It was given to be a museum in 1929 by Dr Marie Stopes, the pioneer of birth control, who lived on the island. Part of it is in **Avice's Cottage**, built 1640, and later named after the three Avices in Hardy's *The Well-Beloved*. Outside are lumps of petrified wood; inside many interesting exhibits of Portland's history. Opposite is the entrance to multi-towered **Pennsylvania Castle** built in 1800 for John Penn, grandson of William Penn, the founder of Pennsylvania, USA, once Governor of Portland. It is now a hotel.

Turn left down Church Ope Road under the bridge of **Rufus** or **Bow and Arrow Castle**, a fifteenth century ruin on the site of an earlier castle. The path right passes an open area overlooking the inhospitable shore, a boulder-strewn plain raised from the sea. Follow steps down towards **Church Ope Cove**, a sheltered haven, once the main place for landing fish and for loading stone barges and smuggling. Today it is a quiet pleasure beach. Where the path turns sharp left turn right up stone steps to the ruins of **St Andrew's Church**, the oldest church on the island, parish church of Portland until 1756. Pennsylvania Castle hangs above this deserted place; pass beneath arch up to right of castle and so to main road again. Turn left to continue on the road for just over half a mile, where take track on left down to **Freshwater Bay** and its disused quarries. The Coastal Path has now rejoined the route which stays near the sea until **Portland Bill**, passing **Cave Hole**, a blow-hole at the back of one of the caves. It once spouted water before iron bars were fixed across it.

Continue past beach huts and then above a sea cave to arrive at the 135 foot high red and white lighthouse at the Bill, built in 1905 to replace an earlier one. It is open for viewing between 11 a.m. and 4.30 p.m. from the beginning of August to the end September except Fridays and Saturdays. Winter times need checking. On the plateau nearby are cafes and huts. Jutting out from the land to the west of the lighthouse are ledges of stone, one of which, **Pulpit Rock**, is joined to the land by a man-made slab. The 'TH' of the nearby pyramidal sea-mark stands for Trinity House rather than Thomas Hardy as is often assumed. Half a mile south is the treacherous **Portland Race**, an area of turbulent sea which extends for between two to four miles.

Or by night-moths of measureless size,
And in softness and smoothness well-nigh beyond hearing
Of corporal things.

The souls discover that they are judged at home not by their glorious deeds in war but by their previous everyday lives .

XIV
... Those whose record was lovely and true
Bore to northward for home: those of bitter traditions
Again left the land,

XV
And, towering to seaward in legions,
They paused at a spot
Overbending the Race –
That engulphing, ghast, sinister place –
Whither headlong they plunged, to the fathomless regions
Of myriads forgot.

ST GEORGE REFORNE

Pierston approaches the churchyard during the funeral of Avice Caro:

Against the stretch of water, where a school of mackerel twinkled in the afternoon light, was defined, in addition to the distant lighthouse, a church with its tower, standing about a quarter of a mile off, near the edge of the cliff. The churchyard gravestones could be seen in profile against the same vast spread of watery babble and unrest.

Among the graves moved the form of a man clothed in a white sheet, which the wind blew and flapped coldly every now and then. Near him moved six men bearing a long box, and two or three persons in black followed. The coffin, with its twelve legs, crawled across the isle, while around and beneath it the flashing light from the sea and the school of mackerel were reflected; a fishing-boat, far out in the Channel, being momentarily discernible under the coffin also.

Continue north on Coast Path right of what was once an Admiralty Research Establishment but is now business units. Pass the old **Upper Lighthouse** (1869) where Dr Marie Stopes lived in the 1920s visited by Hardy towards the end of his life. Marie Stopes's ashes were scattered off the Bill in 1958. East is another older lighthouse, opened as a bird sanctuary by Sir Peter Scott in 1961.

The west coast of Portland is wild, dangerous and magnificent. The sea smashes against sheer rocky cliffs which have been the scene of many shipwrecks; even the names of the bays have a desperate ring: **Hallelujah, Wallsend, Mutton Cove** and above all, the notorious **Dead Man's Bay**, off Chesil Beach.

Right of the path are medieval strip fields divided by grass causeways called balks. This system of farming is rare having survived from before land enclosure. Continue along cliff across open space to left of housing estate to the headland of **Blacknor**, where leave Coast Path to turn inland near the base of a small fort. The guns here were silenced in April 1944 as more than 600 American soldiers and seamen drowned in the water below. Because of the number of men in the sea, the coast guns could not fire on the German E-boats that had run amok amid a convoy heading for an invasion exercise at Slapton Sands, South Devon.

Bear left towards road where turn left to the redundant church of **St George Reforne**, high and impressive in its cliff-top churchyard, with line upon line of gravestones, some of which commemorate victims of shipwrecks. The mid-eighteenth century church has an unusual exterior but inside is classical Georgian. Parish church of Portland after the closure of St Andrew's, it has been redundant since 1917, although since restored. Now administered by The Churches Conservation Trust, it is open to the public all year round, in summer from 10.00 a.m. to 5.00 p.m. and in winter from 10-3.

Cross to the other side of the **Weston** road to near corner of the road opposite church, where stands the **George Inn**, one of the oldest occupied houses on Portland. A plaque over the door reveals that this was the home of the Parish Clerk where the ancient Court Leet of the Manor of Portland (a local government body) met. Return to church and turn right

THE STEEP PATH BETWEEN TOP O' HILL AND UNDERHILL

Even the young Pierston finds this steep as he returns home with Avis:

They climbed homeward slowly by the Old Road, Pierston dragging himself up the steep by the wayside hand-rail and pulling Avice after him upon his arm. At the top they turned and stood still. To the left of them the sky was streaked like a fan with the lighthouse rays, and under their front, at periods of a quarter of a minute, there arose a deep hollow stroke like the single beat of a drum, the intervals being filled with a long-drawn rattling, as of bones between huge canine jaws. It came from the vast concave of Deadman's Bay, rising and falling against the pebble dyke.

Small fishing boats between Portland and Weymouth near Sandsfoot Castle, *on the verge of the ragstone cliff,* which was built by King Henry VIII as a fort to protect shipping. Drawing: S. Prout. Engraved by George Cooke

to Fortuneswell. After a few yards turn left into quarry entrance towards the sea and bear right to rejoin Coast Path. The next stretch of the walk is amazing, partly because of the outstanding view west along Chesil Beach and also because of the unique character of the cliff-path, through a landscape dominated by huge blocks of stone lying at random where discarded by quarrymen. The path, fortified by these in places, passes between intimidating stone bastions. This is **The Tout Quarry Sculpture Park** with sculptures in Portland stone. In summer the rare Silver Studded Blue Butterfly can be seen.

There are plans to create a mass extinction monitoring observatory here, the **MEMO** project, with the objective of halting man's desecration of other species and the environment.

The cliffs show signs of subsidence which is affecting the coastal path; inland diversion is necessary so follow signs.

As Chiswell appeared ahead sounds of the Martinmas Fair drifted up to me. This late autumn event dates back to at least the thirteenth century. Originally a sheep and cattle fair, when these were ferried over from the mainland, today it is entertainment. Below are the narrow terraced streets of **Chiswel**l between Dead Man's Bay and Fortuneswell, which suffered serious flooding in 1979. The flood sirens were sounded early in 2014 when the sea breached Chesil Beach at Fortuneswell. When Hardy visited Portland in 1879 a woman told him that in the November gale of 1824, which struck in the early hours of the morning, her house was destroyed and several people drowned. In fact 30 people were drowned that night.

Follow the coast path signs (and diversion) down into Fortuneswell then the path back over the Causeway.

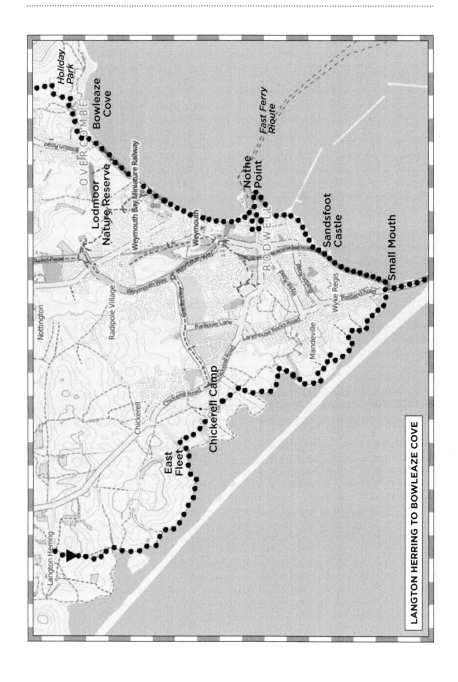

LANGTON HERRING TO BOWLEAZE COVE

FROM PORTLAND TO OWERMOIGNE

Back across the causeway at Ferrybridge, follow concrete path to the right. Join track of the dismantled Weymouth to Portland railway for nearly a mile to the ruins of **Sandsfoot Castle**, already mentioned in connection with Portland Castle. Coastal erosion has drastically undermined Sandsfoot, which housed a Royal Mint during Royalist occupation in the Civil War. Fragments of medieval stonework found in the ruins are believed to have originated in Bindon Abbey, Wool. There is a garden and café.

Follow the road above the castle for a short distance before joining the Coastal Path around the shore of Portland Harbour, across the **Nothe Gardens** to the **Nothe Fort**. A Napoleonic defence on the site was replaced by the present building between 1860-72, the period during which the Verne Citadel was built. Here, too, convict labour was used. Both became known as Palmerston Follies, ordered by the Prime Minister of the time but not used for their primary purpose. Nothe was modernised in 1905 and was an observation point with anti-aircraft guns in the Second World War. There is a new promenade by the shore with low relief sculpted Jurassic fossils. Around Nothe Point is the Severn Lifeboat, the Royal National Lifeboat Institution's largest boat.

You can take a ferry across **Weymouth Harbour**, once the headquarters of a large fleet of paddle-steamers operated by Weymouth, Bournemouth and Swanage Steam Packets Ltd. These were pleasure boats integral to the holiday scene along this part of the south coast for over a hundred years until the 1960s. They also crossed the Channel to Cherbourg. In 1882 the Hardys went to Cherbourg from Weymouth and two years later Hardy accompanied his brother, Henry, to the Channel Islands from here.

The fast ferry operated between Weymouth and the Channel Islands will cease from Easter 2015 to be replaced by a more streamlined one from Poole. The harbour is now used for fishing and as a yachting marina with an annual regatta in May.

WEYMOUTH/BUDMOUTH

SANDSFOOT CASTLE/HENRY THE EIGHTH'S CASTLE

In *The Well-Beloved* Jocelyn Pierston hoped that Avice Caro would walk along the beach with him to the castle on the evening when he left the Isle of Slingers. Avice's decision not to do so was governed by her fear that such an assignation would make people think that she and Jocelyn had adhered to the Island custom of trial marriage, which in the past had tested a woman's fertility to reproduce true Portland stock. In the event it is Marcia Bencomb who walks past the *ruined castle* with him after the storm.

NOTHE FORT/LOOK-OUT

This is mentioned several times in Hardy's work. In *The Melancholy Hussar* of *Wessex Tales* the young German Matthaus Tina and his friend, Christophe, try to escape from service in King George's German Legion by rowing from the harbour to the **Nothe** and from there across the Channel to France. They mistake Jersey for the mainland, are seized by the authorities as deserters and executed by a firing party on their return to Weymouth.

In *The Dynasts*, Hardy's epic poem set at the time of the Napoleonic wars, the Nothe serves its true purpose as a great semi-underground fortress.

In *A Few Crusted Characters*, a story from the collection *Life's Little Ironies*, the strange tale of the Hardcomes relates how disaster strikes two young engaged couples holidaying in Budmouth and seen walking on the Look-out.

THE HARBOUR

In *Desperate Remedies* Owen and Cytherea Graye take

> *A very popular local excursion by steamboat to Lulwind Cove ... announced through the streets of Budmouth one Thursday morning by the weak-voiced town-crier, to start at six o'clock the same day.*

Bob Loveday, in *The Trumpet Major*, looks at

> *the busy scene of loading and unloading craft and swabbing the decks of yachts; at the boats and barges rubbing against the quay wall, and at the houses of the merchants, some ancient structures of solid stone, others green-shuttered with heavy wooden bow-windows which appeared as if about to drop into the harbour by their own weight.*

Continue along the quay towards **Town Bridge** past Hope Street and **Brewers Quay**, a tourist complex with a Timewalk Weymouth history experience and speciality shopping village. A turning to the left, Trinity Street, is worth investigating. The Old Rooms Inn on the left was an assembly room in the eighteenth century. Press gangs operated here at the time of the Napoleonic Wars. There are many pre-eighteenth century buildings including two late sixteenth century stone houses with mullioned windows. One of these, **Tudor House**, is open to the public. Along the quay are attractive bow-fronted houses. Trinity Church, on the south side of Town Bridge, replaced Wyke Regis as the parish church of Weymouth in the 1830s and was enlarged in 1887. On the north side of the harbour are the brick Custom House and the Harbour Master's office in Portland stone, both built in the early nineteenth century.

Cross the bridge, built in 1930, the sixth since the first timber structure, which had seventeen arches and a drawbridge in the 1590s. There were two separate medieval ports on either side of the River Wey: **Weymouth** on the south side and **Melcombe Regis** on the north. These became one by order of Queen Elizabeth I in 1571 and took the name Weymouth. The ancient High Street was destroyed in the Second World War.

There are two Weymouths, winter and summer, quite different from each other: in winter, quieter, more leisurely: in summer, bustling, noisy, packed with tourists. It is interesting that the town was a fashionable holiday resort by the end of the eighteenth century whereas Bournemouth, now comparatively enormous, had only a couple of dozen buildings as late as the mid-nineteenth.

George III was responsible for Weymouth's popularity from 1789. He took a fancy to the place and stayed here for fourteen family holidays until 1805 when his health deteriorated. His brother, the Duke of Gloucester, built **Gloucester Lodge** in 1780, the first house in Weymouth to face the sea. It became the **Gloucester Hotel**, on the Esplanade, but is now flats. The King stayed at the Lodge, went sea-bathing from a horse-drawn bathing machine, rode, sailed on excursions in ships of the Royal Navy, visited local great houses, attended the theatre and reviewed his troops. He gave status to Weymouth and the town showed its gratitude by erecting the great statue at the western end of the sea-front to mark the fiftieth year

It was in this area that the Hardys stayed on their holiday in 1879. The weather was wet, as vividly described in *The Life*:

the steamer-bell ringing persistently, and nobody going on board except an unfortunate boys' school that had come eight miles by train that morning to spend a happy day by the sea. The rain goes into their baskets of provisions, and runs out a strange mixture of cake-juices and mustard-water, but they try to look as if they were enjoying it – all except the pale thin assistant-master who has come with them, and whose face is tragic with his responsibilities. The Quay seems quite deserted till, on going along it, groups of boatmen are discovered behind each projecting angle of the wall – martyrs in countenance, talking of what their receipts would have been if the season had turned out fine; and the landladies' faces at every lodging-house window watching the drizzle and the sea it half obscures.

In *The Mayor of Casterbridge* the sailor, Newson, feels the necessity to live by the sea:

The contiguity of salt water proved to be such a necessity of his existence that he preferred Budmouth as a place of residence, notwithstanding the society of his daughter in the other town. Thither he went, and settled in lodgings in a green-shuttered cottage which had a bow-window, jutting out sufficiently to afford glimpses of a vertical strip of blue sea to any one opening the sash, and leaning forward far enough to look through a narrow lane of tall intervening houses.

This sounds like the harbour area!

THE OLD ROOMS INN

In *The Dynasts* this is where the boatmen and burghers discuss Nelson's death at Trafalgar and how his body was brought home preserved *in a cask of sperrits* which the sailors had to broach as they had run out of grog!

A short story set in **Budmouth** in 1802-03, just after the French Revolution, tells how *A Committee Man of 'The Terror'* and a young aristocratic lady are thrown together as two strangers in a foreign country. He lodges in the **Old Rooms Inn**.

of his reign. Queen Victoria did not have to do much to earn her statue; she visited only once and briefly in 1846; the bronze statue in the middle of the road at the north end of the Esplanade was erected when she died in 1901. The cast-iron clock with its illuminated face commemorates her Golden Jubilee in 1887. This used to be on the sands but since land reclamation has graduated to the Esplanade.

The **Esplanade** is Weymouth's glory. It curves round the bay, a marvellous display of terraced Georgian and Victorian houses, many with bow windows, some now hotels, **Bay Royal, Victoria, Prince Regent**, the names personify the elegance they once exuded. Many of them are now wine bars, arcades and B & Bs. The wide, sandy beach offers all the usual seaside attractions in the summer season. In the past naval fleets were reviewed in the Bay, which is over two miles long to Redcliffe Point in the east.

It seems impossible that such a place could have been where the terrible Black Death, the bubonic and pneumonic plague, entered the country in 1348, as a result of which some thirty to fifty percent of the population of the British Isles was wiped out.

Weymouth has many associations with Hardy. He visited as a child with his father in a horse-drawn transport. In 1869 he worked with local architect G.R. Crickmay on church restoration and lodged at **3, Wooperton Street**, a small road which links Commercial Road and Park Street, which lie a block behind Royal Terrace. Hardy thoroughly enjoyed his time in Weymouth, which was then a lively garrison town. He swam and rowed in the bay near Preston, on the east side, and afterwards wrote that his health improved so much that physically he went back ten years in his age *almost as by the touch of an enchanter's wand*. He also went to the theatre, attended a quadrille (dancing) class and musical performances at the Royal Hotel Assembly Rooms. It was during this time that he is believed to have had a close relationship with his cousin, Tryphena Sparks. In 1871-72 he returned to supervise the building of Church schools at Broadwey, north of the town, and Radipole, north of Radipole Lake, now a bird sanctuary, once a Roman port and the site of army barracks from 1795-1804. He lodged this time at 1, West Parade, now **Park Street**, and began writing *Desperate Remedies*, his first published novel, 1871. In 1897 he came with Emma for a

TOWN BRIDGE/HARBOUR BRIDGE

This is how Hardy describes a previous bridge, built in 1824 in stone, with an iron-swinging central section:

> *From here, the quay, one looks above to mark*
> *The bridge across the harbour, hanging dark*
> *Against the day's-end sky, fair-green in glow*
> *Over and under the middle archway's bow:*
> *It draws its skeleton where the sun has set,*
> *Yea, clear from cutwater to parapet;*
> *On which mild glow, too, lines of rope and spar*
> Trace themselves black as char.

THE ESPLANADE AND BAY

Set at the time of the Napoleonic Wars, *The Trumpet-Major* contains many descriptions of Budmouth while King George III was in residence:

> *The popular Georgian watering-place was in a paroxysm of gaiety. The town was quite overpowered by the country round, much to the town's delight and profit. The fear of invasion was such that six frigates lay in the roads to ensure the safety of the royal family, and from the regiments of horse and foot quartered at the barracks, or encamped on the hills round about, a picket of a thousand men mounted guard every day in front of Gloucester Lodge ...*

Anne Garland and the Loveday brothers watch the King return from a cruise in his yacht:

> *By the time they reached the pier it was six o'clock; the royal yacht was returning; a fact announced by the ships in the harbour firing a salute. The King came ashore with his hat in his hand, and returned the salutations of the well-dressed crowd in his old indiscriminate fashion ... joined the Queen and princesses at Gloucester Lodge, the homely house of red brick in which he unostentatiously resided.*

Bob Loveday watches a royal sea-bathing session:

> *The royal bathing-machine had been drawn out just as Bob reached Gloucester Buildings, and he waited a minute ... to look on. Immediately that the King's machine had entered the water a group of florid men with fiddles, violoncellos, a trombone, and a drum, came forward, packed themselves into another machine that was in waiting, and were drawn out into the waves in the King's*

Weymouth Harbour looking towards the sea. Many old buildings remain on both sides of the water. The southern side became less fashionable with the development of the Esplanade in Melcombe Regis. Drawing: Douglas Snowdon

The bathing machine with the Royal Coat of Arms used by King George III on his first visits to Weymouth. It was horse-drawn into the sea. Later versions, more sophisticated, actually floated. Source: Rodney Legg collection

rear. All that was to be heard for a few minutes were the slow pulsations of the sea; and then a deafening noise burst from the interior of the second machine with power enough to spilt the boards asunder; it was the condensed mass of musicians inside, striking up the strains of 'God save the King' as his Majesty's head rose from the water.

In *The Dynasts* Budmouth beach is eulogised by a sergeant serving in Spain who sings nostalgically of the fine times that the soldiers had when stationed back home:

When we lay where Budmouth Beach is,
O, the girls were fresh as peaches,
With their tall and tossing figures and their eyes of blue and brown!
And our hearts would ache with longing
As we paced from our sing-songing,
    With a smart Clink! Clink! up the Esplanade and down.

Further along the **Esplanade** from **Gloucester Lodge** is 13, Belvidere, the **Belvedere Hotel** where Cytherea was interviewed by her future employer, Miss Aldclyffe.

Hardy recalled his own memories of Weymouth in *At a Seaside Town in 1869*. This had a sub-title *(Young Lover's Reverie)* and may refer to his relationship with Tryphena Sparks. It is vividly evocative of the town's atmosphere:

The boats, the sands, the esplanade,
The laughing crowd;
Light-hearted, loud
Greetings from some not ill-endowed;

The evening sunlit cliffs, the talk,
Hailings and halts,
The keen sea-salts,
The band, the Morgenblatter Waltz.

The Morgenblatter Waltz is by Johann Strauss II and Hardy had heard it played by the town band.

It is not surprising that the novel he was writing during his stay in Weymouth at this time, *Desperate Remedies*, should have the town as one of its main settings. Owen Graye works for an architect, as did Hardy himself. Owen and his sister,

holiday and his mother visited and accompanied them on some excursions. It was during this time that he wrote *The Trumpet Major*. One of his last visits was nearly fifty years later when he watched a dramatisation of *The Mayor of Casterbridge* by John Drinkwater in a *flying matinée*.

Leave Weymouth either by the beach or along the sea wall in front of the **Lodmoor Country Park Nature Reserve**. You can divert on to a gravel path on the landward side of a cycle path in the RSPB Reserve to view the rich bird life in season, including common terns, little egrets, maybe a heron and winter waders. Turn right back to the promenade along Beechdown Way then left to **Overcombe**, where the road turns inland. Take the minor road that forks right up a hill. Just past the Spyglass Inn bear right up a grassy hill to the top of Furzy Cliff with views back across Lodmoor. Ahead at **Bowleaze Cove** is a vast hotel complex. Continue down the greensward towards this to join a road at the bottom straight ahead past two sets of brick traffic calming pillars. Opposite exit of the car park of The Riviera Hotel on the right take a footpath left just past the main entrance to The Waterside Holiday Park on the left. The footpath sign is hidden in a high hedge opposite a fence. Follow private road through the holiday park until a sharp right-hand bend near willow trees. Follow right to near the top of an incline where turn left near a calor gas storage area. Cross stile to lane. Turn left for about half a mile to **St Andrews** the parish church of Preston and Sutton Poyntz, whose sixteenth century tower stands high in a sea of modern development and caravans. Built in local limestone, it is approached through an impressive wooden lych-gate. Inside is evidence of strong interest in campanology with many certificates of striking achievements. One of the stained glass windows shows scenes from John Bunyan's *The Pilgrim's Progress*.

Cross the busy main road to Sutton Road which leads to **Sutton Poyntz**, a delightful village that has succumbed to waves of modern development. The heart of the place is still recognisable but it has become a dormitory for Weymouth and Dorchester and a retirement haven. Take the right-hand fork to a willow-fringed former millpond alive with a variety of ducks. **The Springhead Inn** offers refreshment. A cottage on the left is dated 1683. Beyond in a Georgian house is the **Museum of Water Supply** housed in a pumping station which still supplies water to Weymouth. You can see a medieval dam and an 1857 turbine pump.

Cytherea, lodge at 3, Cross Street; Hardy lodged at 3, Wooperton Street. Edward Springrove and Cytherea, rowing in the bay, see the

distant Esplanade, now with its line of houses, lying like a dark grey band against the light western sky ... She surveyed the long line of lamps on the sea-wall of the town, now looking small and yellow, and seeming to send long tap-roots of fire quivering down deep into the sea.

The poem *On the Esplanade* projects a similar image:

The horizon gets lost in a mist new-wrought by the night:
The lamps of the Bay
That reach from behind me round to the left and right
On the sea-wall way
For a constant mile of curve, make a long display
As a pearl-strung row,
Under which in the waves they bore their gimlets of light:– ...

Perhaps the most convincing accolade of the town is given by Diggory Venn, the reddleman in *The Return of the Native*. He extols its virtues to Eustacia Vye, who agrees with him:

'Now Budmouth is a wonderful place – wonderful – a great salt sheening sea bending into the land like a bow – thousands of gentle people walking up and down – bands of music playing – officers by sea and officers by land walking among the rest – out of every ten folk you meet nine of 'em in love.'
'I know it,' she said disdainfully. 'I know Budmouth better than you. I was born there.... Ah, my soul, Budmouth! I wish I was there now.'

LODMOOR

In the nineteenth century there was horse-racing at **Lodmoor**. In *Far From the Madding Crowd* Frank Troy loses more than £100 in a month soon after his marriage to Bathsheba. Like most gamblers he looks for excuses:

'The fact is, these autumn races are the ruin of everybody. Never did I see such a day as 'twas! 'Tis a wild open place, just out of Budmouth, and a drab sea rolled in towards us like liquid misery ... Horses, riders, people, were all blown about like ships at sea, ...'

Booking required. To book an appointment on 01305 832634.
Admission free.

From the Springhead turn right along a No Through Lane to a gate. Follow straight ahead along hedge until the third left path on a diagonal up the field in the direction of **King George** and his White Horse. Cut in the chalk in 1808, it is 280 feet long by 323 feet high. The King objected to the fact that he is depicted riding away from Weymouth! It has to be 'scoured' at regular intervals to prevent grass growing over it. King George's troops camped on the **Ridgeway** near here. There is a stile in the corner by the wood; follow path straight on through wood and up, keeping the White Horse on the left, to a track that runs along the edge of a large field. Turn right to follow a splendid ridge bridleway along **White Horse Hill** for about one-and-a-half miles to Poxwell, passing tumuli on the seaward side with good views back along the coast to Portland and eastwards to the headland of White Nothe.

Turn inland from the coast to **Poxwell Manor**, with its distinctive cluster of no less than twelve Elizabethan chimneys. Built in Portland stone, it has a brick walled garden and a small arched gateway with a porter's lodge over it. It's a private house with the thick conifer hedge at the front ensuring privacy.

Turn left through the tiny village of Poxwell to pass four pairs of thatched stone cottages built in 1843. Cross road to turn right through gate and up field near hedge with a glimpse of the beech clump on the roundabout at Warmwell Cross to the left and views across 'Egdon Heath' and Winfrith as you climb. Go through gateway to right at top of field, turn left to head for barn. Go left through gate just before barn then right through further gate to pass left of barn downhill. At bottom approach ruined barn but turn left, right onto track then left on chalk track up shallow valley, with **Moigns Down** on the right. Pass through gate at top of hill then turn sharp left to double stile in corner. Follow straight hedge straight ahead with a good view of Warmwell Manor ahead to the left. I walked here in October through Michaelmas daisies towards large clump of russet beeches on a hill. Cross the busy A352 to track which leads to a small-holding. Take overgrown path to the right before the buildings over stile to the village hall in **Owermoigne** from which a concrete path leads to road.

PRESTON/CRESTON

In the story *A Changed Man* which is about the cholera epidemic in Casterbridge in 1854, Laura Maumbury, wife of the curate of Durnover parish, is evacuated to **Creston** and meets Lieutenant Vannicock from Budmouth infantry barracks.

SUTTON POYNTZ/OVERCOMBE

In the parish church Bob Loveday and Anne Garland attend afternoon service to find that army recruits from nearby hamlets have been drilling outside the churchyard gate. Inside are stored the pikes used by this 'Dad's Army'.

Descriptions of the mill in *The Trumpet Major* are mainly from Hardy's imagination, but include details of two mills that existed in **Sutton Poyntz** early in the nineteenth century. The existing mill was not there in Napoleonic times, but is on the site of the original Lower Mill. The Upper Mill was demolished in 1856. This is the view from Anne's window:

Immediately before her was the large, smooth mill-pond, over-full, and intruding into the hedge and into the road. The water, with its flowing leaves and spots of froth, was stealing away, like Time, under the dark arch, to tumble over the great slimy wheel within. On the other side of the mill-pond was an open place called the Cross, because it was three-quarters of one, two lanes and a cattle-drive meeting there ... Behind this a steep slope rose high into the sky, merging in a wide and open down, now littered with sheep newly shorn. The upland by its height completely sheltered the mill and village from north winds, making summer of springs, reducing winters to autumn temperatures, and permitting myrtle to flourish in the open air.

THE RIDGEWAY

King George III and his retinue pass along here on their way to Budmouth and it is where he reviews his troops one morning watched by *Everybody Great and Small* from Overcombe. For a short time the usually quiet hills become alive with colour and movement but

by one o'clock the downs were again bare.
  They still spread their grassy surface to the sun ... but the King and his fifteen thousand armed men, the horses, the bands of music, the princesses, the cream-coloured teams ... how entirely have they all passed and gone!

Some time after, John Loveday takes Anne to watch the chalk figures of King George and his horse being excavated on the hillside.

The village is only a stone's throw from the A352 but remains unspoiled. New houses are contained in the west part of the village leaving the area around the church tranquil and mellow. Owermoigne has a history of smuggling. Contraband was landed along the coast between Weymouth and Lulworth, in Ringstead Bay for example, and transported inland by the smuggling fraternity which included people from all walks of life. Indeed the church of **St Michael** was involved; the small fifteenth century tower was used as a store, as was the rectory further along **Church Lane** on the right, which has a bricked-up window believed to have been used for receiving casks of brandy. During the first half of the nineteenth century the authorities clamped down on smuggling. In 1849 the Rev. S.G. Osborne wrote: 'Smuggling gave a very large amount of employment to the peasantry of this county, and, directly and indirectly, put a great deal of money in their way.'

He suggested that its suppression was one of the causes of the poverty of the labourer in the nineteenth century.

The **Rectory** is mostly Elizabethan and has beams in the dining room taken from a wreck of the Spanish Armada in Ringstead Bay.

Dorset's last living link to Thomas Hardy was broken in October 2011 with the death at the age of 105 in Owermoigne of Norrie Woodall who had acted in the original Hardy Players in the 1920s at Hardy's home, Max Gate, Dorchester in which her sister, Gertrude, played the part of Tess. In 2005 Norrie reformed the theatrical group and returned to the stage at the age of 100. Subsequently she campaigned with institutions such as the University of Exeter and Dorset County Museum to raise £58,000 to keep a collection of Hardy's work in the United Kingdom. Norrie lived in Owermoigne for many years and once had a chicken farm here.

In the lane that leads to the village hall opposite the church is an old pump with a notice that proclaims: 'Traction engines are not allowed water from this pump.'

The hexagonal brick gatehouse of Poxwell (pronounced 'Pokeswell')
Manor. It was constructed in 1634. The Manor was built by the
Henning family, merchants of Poole. Drawing: Douglas Snowdon

The mill pond at Sutton Poyntz overlooked by a line of thatched cottages. White Horse Down is in the background. Drawing: Douglas Snowdon

The grey-gabled Stafford House, West Stafford. Its grounds still include the shrubberies and plantations along the back of the Froom mentioned in The Waiting Supper. Engraving: J.H. LeKeux, 1863

POXWELL MANOR/OXWELL HALL

In *The Trumpet-Major* this is the home of the miserly Benjamin Derriman, who leaves it to Anne when he dies. It was very run-down and dilapidated then *with its muddy quadrangle, archways, mullioned windows, cracked battlements, and weed-grown garden.* The path that descends to the house from the downs behind it is where John and Anne heard boisterous noises and discovered the irresponsible Festus Derriman merry-making with his friends from the yeomanry cavalry.

WARMWELL CROSS/WARM'ELL CROSS

In *The Distracted Preacher* from *Wessex Tales* the smugglers ambush the excisemen and tie them to the trees at **Warm'ell Cross**.

OWERMOIGNE/NETHER MOYNTON

The Distracted Preacher is said to be based on actual events that happened in the area around **Owermoigne** between 1825-30.

Lizzy Newberry, the young widow much involved in smuggling, lives in a thatched cottage in **Church Lane**, east of the church, nearly opposite the **Rectory**. She takes the young Wesleyan minister, Stockdale, through her garden and across a wall to the church tower to draw off some brandy to help cure his cold. An information sheet in the church describes smuggling in the village.

Lizzy warns the lugger bringing the contraband of danger by burning furze on the headland of **White Nothe**, which she reaches by crossing the turnpike road (the present A352) and following the track, now a minor road, via Holworth towards Ringworth Bay (Ringstead). Her second more productive journey with the other smugglers is across Shaldon Down (Chaldon) to Dagger's Grave (Dagger's Gate) to Lulwind.

When the excisemen search the village all the male villagers hide in the church tower to avoid having to assist them:

All the missing parishioners, lying on their stomachs on the tower roof, except a few who, elevated on their hands and knees, were peeping through the embrasures of the parapet. Stockdale did the same, and saw the village lying like a map below him, over which moved the figures of the Customs-men, each foreshortened to a crablike object, the crown of his hat forming a circular disc in the centre of him.

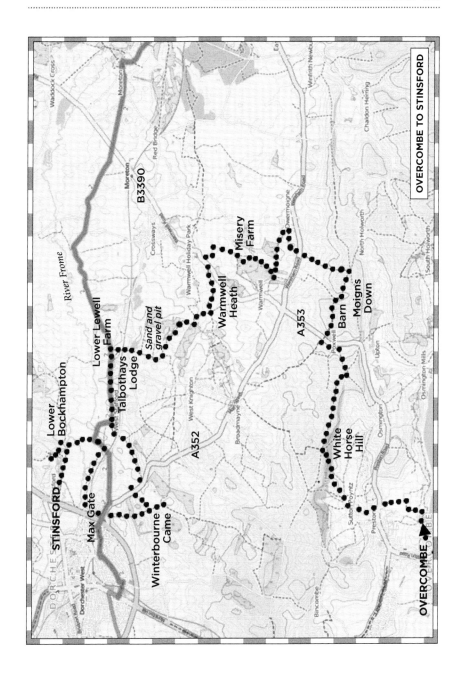

The orchard where the seventy tubs of spirits were secreted can be found alongside the churchyard west of the tower adjoining a modern bungalow. The forge where the unwilling blacksmith repairs the sabotaged carts is today a single-storey private house on the corner of Holland's Mead Avenue.

BETWEEN WARMWELL HEATH AND THE RIVER FROME/FROOM

In the early 1890s when Hardy was writing *Tess*, which is set earlier in the century, the sand and gravel pits were far less extensive than they are today. They are mentioned just once in the novel, when Tess and Angel journey from Talbothays in the Froom Valley to a farmhouse *on the slopes above the vale* to check the progress of the cows about to calve. They return via *a great gravel-cliff* immediately over the levels. Hardy seems to have moved this north, which would not amuse the inhabitants of the valley villages today!

LOWER LEWELL FARM/TALBOTHAYS DAIRY

Tess first arrives at **Talbothays** as the cows are called in for milking:

> *Tess followed slowly in their rear, and entered the barton by the open gate through which they had entered before her. Long thatched sheds stretched round the enclosure, their slopes encrusted with vivid green moss, and their eaves supported by wooden posts rubbed to a glossy smoothness by the flanks of infinite cows and calves of bygone years, now passed to an oblivion almost inconceivable in its profundity.*

The group of buildings includes a seventeenth century farmhouse and a later dairy-house and thatched brick barn that abuts on the road. The dairy-house has two storeys, the upper of which fits the description of Angel Clare's bedroom, *an immense attic which ran the whole length of the dairy-house.* The position of the farm in relation to the Frome accords well with Hardy's evocative images of the *open mead* where Tess and Angel walk in the early morning to where the cows lie:

> *At these non-human hours they could get quite close to the waterfowl. Herons came, with a great bold noise as of opening doors and shutters, out of the boughs of a plantation which they frequented at the side of the mead; ...*

> *They could then see the faint summer fogs in layers, woolly, level, and apparently no thicker than counterpanes ...*

FROM OWERMOIGNE TO STINSFORD

Leave the village opposite the church past the old pump. Near end of track take the path for Warmwell to the right initially up a flight of steps. Go through gap in corner of field to further gap then along fence straight ahead to corner of field where path enters wood. Over first stile bear left over footbridge and follow path through wood then ahead to top of field where turn right towards gate on edge of wood into young plantation. Do not go through gate from where there is a good view of Warmwell Manor but turn right down field parallel with wood to corner. Cross stile and field turning left to avoid farm complex keeping to the left of lake on a new permissive diversion at the end of which turn right on to tarmac drive turning left just before buildings in front of beautifully converted barn, Misery Farm. Follow track straight on for about three-quarters of a mile where the drive comes to the B3390 between Warmwell and Crossways.

Turn left for a short way to a bridleway on the right over **Warmwell Heath**, also **The Jubilee Trail**, sandy and fern-lined, for three-quarters of a mile to cross tracks where turn right, leaving the Jubilee Trail . Climb to left of house past watercress beds to bear left up hill onto narrow path. At T junction turn left towards electricity pylon with sand and gravel pits on right. Continue along wide bridleway to bear right under power lines to gate next to pylon. Turn left to follow edge of wood then straight on bridleway to metal gate on corner. Here leave main bridleway to turn sharp right across the end of a long field to further gate. This leads to a gravelly route that skirts the West Knighton Sand and Gravel Pits. This area is riddled with these pits and there is much concern in the villages of West Stafford and Woodsford that this industry should not encroach further north into the Frome Valley. Soon pass between hedges straight on to cross lane, railway and further field to **Lower Lewell Farm**. Turn left towards **West Stafford**.

On the right, across the **Frome Valley**, high on Duddle Heath, not far from Higher Bockhampton, are Rainbarrows, three Bronze Age round burial mounds used as a beacon in the past. Hardy often climbed to these when he was young, to gaze across the heath to Dorchester.

RAINBARROWS

In *The Return of the Native* the locals light a bonfire on the beacon to commemorate the Gunpowder Plot:

The first tall flame from Rainbarrow sprang into the sky, attracting all eyes that had been fixed on the distant conflagrations back to their own attempt in the same kind. The cheerful blaze streaked the inner surface of the human circle – now increased by other stragglers, male and female – with its own gold livery, and even overlaid the dark turf around with a lively luminousness, which softened off into obscurity where the barrow rounded downwards out of sight. It showed the barrow to be the segment of a globe, as perfect as on the day when it was thrown up, even the little ditch remaining from which the earth was dug. Not a plough had ever disturbed a grain of that stubborn soil. In the heath's barrenness to the farmer lay its fertility to the historian. There had been no obliteration, because there had been no tending.

TALBOTHAYS LODGE

When Mary Hardy died in 1915 Hardy wrote several poems in memory of her. *In the Garden (M.H.)* recalls a fleeting moment by the sundial at **Talbothays**.

We waited for the sun
To break its cloudy prison
(For day was not yet done,
And night still unbegun)
Leaning by the dial.

After many a trial –
We all silent there –
It burst as new-arisen,
Throwing a shade to where
Time travelled at that minute.

Little saw we in it,
But this much I know,
Of lookers on that shade,
Her towards whom it made
Soonest had to go.

About half-a-mile along on the left is **Talbothays Lodge**, designed by Hardy and built by his brother, Henry, in the 1890s, on farm land owned by their father. Henry and his sisters, Mary and Kate, lived here after leaving Higher Bockhampton in 1914. The word 'hays' means a hedged enclosure. The house is in brick, solid, not beautiful, not really a *country* house. In the garden is a sundial on which are Henry, Mary and Kate's initials. Hardy visited his family most Sunday afternoons over a period of forty years, first at Higher Bockhampton, then at Talbothays, from Max Gate, Dorchester. He cycled until he was over eighty, then walked. His last visit was on 4 November 1927, two months before his death.

Continue on to **West Stafford**. The network of roads around Dorchester threaten the village's tranquillity. As in many such places you can't help feeling that it must have been so much better a hundred or so years ago but people living then would no doubt have envied us for many of the trappings of 'progress'. There is plenty of thatch, including a massive eighteenth century former barn. The church of **St Andrew** dates mainly from the seventeenth century with an earlier tower and Victorian restoration. West Stafford House, north of the village, is best viewed from further along the route. The **Wise Man Inn** stands in the centre of the village.

The last part of the walk is necessarily somewhat tortuous in order to include important Hardy places. I make no apologies!

Go down **Rectory Lane** opposite the church. When the lane ends continue straight on a bridleway to Came Park with stream on right. Curve to the left round the **Old Rectory**, where Hardy dined in 1878. Under the railway bridge cross the road where take the right-hand bridleway straight ahead next to hedge with the **South Winterborne** stream on right. **Frome Hill** can be seen to the right. After three-quarters of a mile the path emerges on the A352. Turn right for one-quarter of a mile where take the lane on the left through park gates into **Winterborne Came Park**. Follow this for another quarter-mile to left turning to **Winterborne Came Church and House**. The poet William Barnes, a friend of Hardy, was rector of **St Peter's Church** from 1862-86 and is buried in the churchyard beneath a large Saxon-style cross, south of the tower. The church is somehow sad, once the heart of a small but live community, now deserted and all but forgotten

WEST STAFFORD/FROOM EVERARD

This is the setting of the story *The Waiting Supper*, which tells of a thwarted romance between Christine Everard, daughter of the squire of Froom-Everard House, and Nicholas Long, a yeoman farmer at nearby Elsenford (Duddle Farm, north-east of Lower Bockhampton). Nicholas returns after a fifteen year absence to find that many of his former acquaintances are buried in the churchyard *side by side as they had lived.*

The church is also the scene of Tess's marriage:

> *As they came out of church the ringers swung the bells off their rests, and a modest peal of three notes broke forth – that limited amount of expression having been deemed sufficient by the church builders for the joys of such a small parish. Passing by the tower with her husband on the path to the gate she could feel the vibrant air humming round them from the louvred belfry in a circle of sound …*

FROME HILL/FROOM HILL

Angel Clare returned this way from Emminster to the

> *detached knoll a mile or two west of Talbothays, whence he again looked into that green trough of sappiness and humidity, the valley of the Var or Froom.*

One of Hardy's last poems, written in August 1927, is about this spot:

SEEING THE MOON RISE

> *We used to go to Froom-hill Barrow*
> *To see the round moon rise*
> *Into the heath-rimmed skies,*
> *Trudging thither by plough and harrow*
> *Up the pathway steep and narrow,*
> *Singing a song.*
> *Now we do not go there. Why?*
> *Zest burns not so high!*
>
> *Latterly we've only conned her*
> *With a passing glance*
> *From window or door by chance,*
> *Hoping to go again, high yonder,*
> *As we used, and gaze, and ponder,*

except for occasional services and pilgrims to the Barnes grave. It is usually open during the day from May to September. Hardy walked here from Max Gate on numerous occasions and visited the grave. Came House is a large mid-eighteenth century Palladian building with a portico, situated in rolling parkland.

Return to the main lane and go straight over to a footpath towards Dorchester up a track to a line of trees on **Conygar Hill**. An avenue of young trees has been planted on either side of the track to replace a previous avenue of elms and chestnuts. Came House is seen to advantage from here. At the top of the hill go through a belt of trees to a junction of paths. Take the right-hand fork across fields towards Max Gate, which can be glimpsed in its sheltering trees on the far side of a busy roundabout. At the bottom of the slope a path to the right leads to the former **Came Rectory**, on the east side of the A352, a small early nineteenth century building with thatched roof, veranda and intricately paned windows. William Barnes lived here until his death and Hardy visited him both before and after the completion of Max Gate in 1885. Divert to see this if you wish but if not carry on to Max Gate which is to the left over the roundabout, on the corner of Syward Road and Alington Avenue.

Max Gate! The birthplace of *The Woodlanders, Tess, Jude* and most of Hardy's finest poems! I was lucky to be able to visit on a National Trust Open Day on a sunny November morning. I expected it to be gloomy and oppressive as it seems from the exterior but was surprised to find the opposite despite the encircling trees. Built on land acquired from the Duchy of Cornwall in the mid-1880s and named after a nearby tollgate keeper called Mack, this substantial Victorian red brick villa was designed by Hardy, constructed by his brother Henry and disliked by Emma! In its exposed position on a knoll outside the town and later surrounded by trees, especially the sombre Austrian pines that Hardy planted to ensure privacy, it is easy to imagine that when he retreated into his study for long periods, Emma felt isolated and neglected. Even Hardy was oppressed by the place at times as he wrote to his friend Edmund Gosse, *Our life here is lonely and cottage-like*. Modern interior decoration has lightened it considerably but it is a badly planned house — not one of the great man's major successes. The room on the first floor where *Tess* and *Jude* were written is horribly dark, synonymous with the latter. And there was no bath until 1920.

Singing a song.
Thitherward we do not go:
Feet once quick are slow!

WINTERBORNE CAME

When William Barnes died Hardy recorded a poignant moment on the
Winterborne-Came path.

THE LAST SIGNAL
(11 OCT 1886)
A MEMORY OF WILLIAM BARNES

Silently I footed by an uphill road
That led from my abode to a spot yew-boughed;
Yellowly the sun sloped low down to westward,
And dark was the east with cloud.

Then, amid the shadow of that livid sad east,
Where the light was least, and a gate stood wide,
Something flashed the fire of the sun that was facing it,
Like a brief blaze on that side.

Looking hard and harder I knew what it meant –
The sudden shine sent from the livid east scene;
It meant the west mirrored by the coffin of my friend there,
Turning to the road from his green,

To take his last journey forth – he who in his prime
Trudged so many a time from that gate athwart the land!
Thus a farewell to me he signalled on his grave-way,
As with a wave of his hand.

MAX GATE

As the twenty-first century approaches, visitors to **Max Gate** may be moved by a
poem from *Late Lyrics:*

THE STRANGE HOUSE
(MAX GATE, A.D. 2000)

'I hear the piano playing –
Just as a ghost might play,'
'–O, but what are you saying?

There were happy times of course, before their relationship soured. Emma held garden parties, there were visitors, walks and cycle rides in the surrounding countryside and, one Christmas Eve (1893), the carol singers arrived with a *harmonium, ... made a charming picture with their lanterns under the tress, the rays diminishing away in the winter mist*. That New Year's Eve the Hardys stood outside the door listening to the muffled peal from the tower of Fordington St George.

After Emma's death in 1912, by which time Hardy was very famous, many more eminent people visited the grand old man of English literature. He married Florence Dugdale in 1914 and she was to act as hostess to some illustrious literati, including Walter de la Mare, Robert Louis Stevenson, Virginia Woolf, H.G.Wells, Rebecca West, John Galsworthy, Siegfried Sassoon, George Bernard Shaw, E.M.Forster, T.E.Lawrence ... the list is formidable and an acknowledgement of Hardy's achievements. The Hardys also received groups, such as the Balliol Players from Oxford, who performed live theatre for them. Hardy died here aged eight-seven on 11 January 1928.

Kate Hardy bought Max gate when Florence died in 1937. The contents of Hardy's study were given to the Dorset County Museum and the room recreated there; it is one of the museum's star attractions today. When Kate died in 1940 she left the house to the National Trust on the understanding that they would acquire the cottage at Higher Bockhampton. Max Gate is open to the public from the beginning of April to the end of October from Wednesday to Sunday and on Bank Holidays from 11a.m. to 5p.m.

The garden perhaps conveys the most personal touch. On the west side, screened from the house by a laurel shrubbery, is a cluster of tiny tombstones. Here lie the Hardys' pets: Emma's many cats, the black setter Moss, and the notorious Wessex. In a 1956 BBC radio broadcast, Lady Cynthia Asquith, once secretary to Sir James Barrie, a friend of Hardy's, recalled a visit to Max Gate in 1921:

'The moment we arrived I was introduced to the most despotic dog guests have ever suffered under. This notorious dog. . . had, I am sure, the longest biting list of any domestic pet . . . the thick tousle of Wessex's unbrushed coat made it impossible to guess which, if any,

There's no piano today;
    Their old one was sold and broken;
        Years past it went amiss.'
'– I heard it, or shouldn't have spoken:
        A strange house, this!

'I catch some undertone here,
        From some one out of sight.'
'– Impossible; we are alone here,
        And shall be through the night.'
'– The parlour-door – what stirred it?'
        '– No one: no soul's in range.'
'But, any how, I heard it,
        And it seems strange!

Seek my own room I cannot –
        A figure is on the stair!'
'– What figure? Nay I scan not
        Any one lingering there.
A bough outside is waving,
        And that's its shade by the moon'.
'– Well, all is strange! I am craving
        Strength to leave soon.'

'– Ah, maybe you've some vision
        Of showings beyond our sphere;
Some sight, sense, intuition
        Of what once happened here?
The house is old; they've hinted
        It once held two love-thralls,
And they may have imprinted
        Their dreams on its walls?

'They were – I think 'twas told me –
        Queer in their works and ways;
The teller would often hold me
        With weird tales of those days.
Some folk can not abide here,
        But we – we do not care
Who loved, laughed, wept, or died here,
        Knew joy, or despair.'

GREETINGS - - - from
Mr. and Mrs. THOMAS HARDY

Max Gate.
Dorchester.   Xmas 1923

Christmas cards sent by the Hardys in the 1920s and Max Gate as it was in Hardy's old age.
The East Turret was added in the 1890s. Source: Rodney Legg collection

Most visitors to the house between 1913 and 1926 were understandably wary of Wessex, that white canine of indeterminate breed. The Hardys treated him as many childless couples treat their pets. He inspired two poems, *A Popular Personage at Home* and, after his death, *Dead 'Wessex' the Dog to the Household*.

Do you think of me at all,
*   Wistful ones?*
Do you think of me at all
*   As if nigh?*
Do you think of me at all
At the creep of evenfall,
Or when the sky-birds call
*   As they fly?*

Do you look for me at times,
*   Wistful ones?*
Do you look for me at times
*   Strained and still?*
Do you look for me at times,
When the hour for walking chimes,
On that grassy path that climbs
*   Up the hill?*

WEST STAFFORD HOUSE/FROOM EVERARD HOUSE

In *The Waiting Supper* it is described as solidly built in *stone in mullioned and transomed Elizabethan style*. The story is set in the mid-nineteenth century before the house was enlarged. Nicholas and Christine meet in 'The Sallows', a willow grove on the banks of the Froom near a waterfall; this is where Christine's long absent husband, Bellston, drowns.

KEEPER'S COTTAGE

Nicholas Long built it for himself so that he could be near Christine in **Froom-Everard House**.

THE FROME/THE FROOM/THE VAR VALLEY/
THE VALLEY OF THE GREAT DAIRIES

In the low-lying area around West Stafford, Lower Bockhampton and Woodsford, further east, the river has two moods: one gentle, idyllic; the other dangerous

breed he was supposed to belong to . . . (He) was specially uninhibited at dinner-time, most of which he spent not under, but on, the table, walking about unchecked, and contesting every single forkful of food on its way from my plate to my mouth.'

One hopes that this is slightly exaggerated, but it is certain that Wessex was spoiled. Florence chided Hardy for giving 'Wessie' goose and plum pudding at Christmas. A difficult dog — owned by an, at times, irascible master, who nevertheless, at the age of eighty-six, carved lovingly and perfectly on the small headstone:

**THE
FAMOUS DOG
WESSEX
August 1913 — 27 Dec. 1926
Faithful, Unflinching**

Leave the house along **Syward Road** parallel with the garden. Hardy's small private exit can be seen in the wall; he often left this way on walks to avoid attention. At the end of the road you can cross straight over the railway but Hardy often turned left along the path leading up to the bridge, a favourite place in his later years, where he saw the trains carrying Portland stone. Over bridge continue down **Smokey Hole Lane** to **Edison Avenue**, turn right then right again to **St George's Road**. The next half-mile is a bit dreary except for the sight of **Louds Mill** on the left behind the wire fence of a compound. There was a fulling mill here from 1590, where cloth was pounded to make it thick and felty. The mill was enlarged in 1825 but has since become redundant and has fallen into disrepair. In the 1970s some of its higher levels were demolished despite efforts by preservationists, but it is still an attractive building. The same cannot be said for the sewage works complex on the right, for which I DO apologise! Pass by hastily to a footpath that leads straight ahead for about half a mile, with stream on left, to the West Stafford to Lower Bockhampton Road. Turn left opposite **Frome Hill Cottage**.

Soon there is a good view across to **West Stafford House** on the right. It was built in 1633 on the site of an earlier house. At times, like other houses in the area, it was a great dairy. Much altered in 1850, Hardy remembered

and threatening. When Tess first arrives here in May she discovers it in its most magnanimous mood:

The Froom waters were clear as the pure River of Life shown to the Evangelist, rapid as the shadow of a cloud, with pebbly shallows that prattled to the sky all day long.

In July heavy thunderstorms *hissed down upon the meads* and flood *the crooked lane leading from their own parish to Mellstock.* This is the lane between West Stafford and Lower Bockhampton, where Angel carries the milkmaids across the floods. *'Who would have expected such a rise in the river in summer-time!'* exclaims Marian.

In October the Froom is again docile and in harmony with the love of Tess and Angel:

Thus, during this October month of wonderful afternoons they roved along the meads by creeping paths which followed the brinks of trickling tributary brooks, hopping across by little wooden bridges to the other side, and back again. They were never out of the sound of some purling weir, whose buzz accompanied their own murmuring, while the beams of the sun, almost as horizontal as the mead itself, formed a pollen of radiance over the landscape. They saw tiny blue fogs in the shadows of trees and hedges, all the time that there was bright sunshine elsewhere ...

Men were at work here and there – for it was the season for 'taking up' the meadows, or digging the little waterways clear for the winter irrigation, and mending their banks where trodden down by the cows. The shovelfuls of loam, black as jet, brought there by the river when it was as wide as the whole valley, were an essence of soils, pounded champaigns of the past, steeped, refined, and subtilized to extraordinary richness, out of which came all the fertility of the mead, and of the cattle grazing there.

The river is in completely different mood a month later, November, in *The Return of the Native*, when Eustacia Yeobright and Damon Wildeve drown in the frothy waters of Shadwater Weir, swollen by heavy rain.

LOWER BOCKHAMPTON/LOWER MELLSTOCK

The old school-house is where Fancy Day was a teacher in *Under the Greenwood Tree*. The Mellstock carol-singers arrive in the middle of the night:

By this time they were crossing to a gate in the direction of the school which, going there with his father and the musicians from Stinsford to play at a Christmas entertainment. Also on the right is **Keeper's Cottage**.

Continue along the road for half a mile northwards to **Bockhampton Bridge**. This stretch of road crosses numerous side-streams of the **Frome** and gives an idea of the nature of the water meadows. In wet weather water flows everywhere and you can see evidence of the old methods of irrigation — the hatches where water was stored to be released by 'drowners', men whose work was quite an art. Along the river between West Stafford and Woodsford, further east, are a number of weirs. Cross the Frome at Bockhampton Bridge in **Lower Bockhampton**. On the left, near the bridge is a withy bed.

Chronologically Lower Bockhampton after Max Gate is out of order in Hardy's life — unavoidable I'm afraid! It's certainly worthwhile to have a look at the village. **Bridge Cottage**, on the right, was the former blacksmith's and inn. At the corner of the first turning to the left is the former Anglican **National School**, started by Julia Martin of Kingston Maurward 'for the education of children of the labouring classes'. Typical Victorian segregation of the classes! She took a special interest in young Thomas and he was fascinated by her. Educated at home until the age of eight, he was the first pupil to enter the school but left a year later to go to school in Dorchester. He excelled at arithmetic and geography but his handwriting was nothing special. The bell still hangs over the porch.

Follow the side road, **Knapwater**, which means on a hill beside a river, across a cattle grid into the grounds of **Kingston Maurward**. On the right is the **Old Manor House**, built in 1591, in stone, with the coat of arms of the Grey family over the porch. Just past this, a few yards up a hill on the right, are the remains of the old barn, once a fine building where the ten-year-old Hardy went to a harvest supper organised by Mrs Martin.

Kingston Maurward House in the park nearby is a large early eighteenth century building in brick, but since encased in stone, after a deprecating remark by George III to the then Pitt owner, a cousin of William Pitt: 'Only brick, Mr Pitt, only brick'! It was occupied by the army during the Second World War, after which its owner sold it to Dorset County Council. It is now the Dorset College of Agriculture and Horticulture. The gardens are often open to the public.

standing on a slight eminence at the junction of three ways, now rose in unvarying and dark flatness against the sky. The instruments were retuned, and all the band entered the school enclosure, enjoined by old William to keep upon the grass.

'Number seventy-eight,' he softly gave out as they formed round in a semicircle, the boys opening the lanterns to get a clearer light, and directing their rays on the books.

Then passed forth into the quiet night an ancient and time-worn hymn, embodying a quaint Christianity in words orally transmitted from father to son through several generations ...

Hardy paid a surprise visit to his old school later in life, but as is so often the case with going back to places full of memories, he afterwards wished that he had not done so:

HE REVISITS HIS FIRST SCHOOL

I should not have shown in the flesh,
    I ought to have gone as a ghost;
It was awkward, unseemly almost,
    Standing solidly there as when fresh,
Pink, tiny, crisp-curled,
    My pinions yet furled
From the winds of the world.

After waiting so many a year
    To wait longer, and go as a sprite
From the tomb at the mid of some night
    Was the right, radiant way to appear;
Not as one wanzing weak
    From life's roar and reek,
His rest still to seek: ...

KINGSTON MAURWARD/KNAPWATER

The old Tudor manor is where the steward, Manston, lived in *Desperate Remedies*, part of Miss Aldclyffe's estate, **Knapwater**:

an Elizabethan fragment, consisting of as much as could be contained under three gables and a cross roof behind ... The mullioned and transomed windows, containing five or six lights, were mostly bricked up to the extent of two or three, and the remaining portion fitted with cottage window-frames carelessly

Return to Bockhampton Bridge, where on the south side is a riverside path to **Stinsford**, which was the old road from Bockhampton to Dorchester and runs straight for over a mile between two backwaters of the Frome. This was one of Hardy's favourite walks throughout his life. A solitary swan glided gracefully beside the path as I left the bridge. On the right you can glimpse Kingston Maurward through the trees. Continue for half a mile to a path on the right to **Stinsford Church**. Enter the churchyard through a gate on its west side. The squat, light grey tower is fourteenth century; the rest of the church dates from the thirteenth to the seventeenth centuries. Inside the Hardy presence is immediate: a plan drawn by Hardy of the old musicians' gallery; you can see where it was by the patches of cement on the floor at the back of the nave and by the gaps in the stonework on each side of the tower where the supporting beams rested. On the west wall there is a memorial brass in Latin (Hardy thought the language would outlast English), to commemorate the services of the Hardy family to church music from 1802-41. Grandfather Hardy was reputedly more interested in music than the sermon, copying tunes when he should have been listening.

In *The Life* Hardy describes an account by his mother in 1892 of how grandfather Hardy and his two sons, Thomas and James, *used to appear passing over the brow of the hill to Stinsford Church on a Sunday morning, three or four years before my birth. They were always hurrying, being rather late, their fiddles and violoncello in green-baize bags under their left arms. They wore top hats, stick-up shirt collars, dark blue coats with great collars and gilt buttons, deep cuffs and black silk 'stocks' or neckerchiefs. Had curly hair, and carried their heads to one side as they walked. My grandfather wore drab cloth breeches and buckled shoes, but his sons wore trousers and Wellington boots.*

A stained glass window in the south aisle, depicting one of Hardy's favourite passages from the Bible, was raised by public subscription as a memorial to him.

In the vaults lie various members of the Grey and Pitt families of Kingston Maurward. An old custom until 1820 was for recent corpses to remain in the nave during Sunday service, and be buried the following week.

inserted, to suit the purpose to which the old place was now applied, it being partitioned out into small rooms downstairs to form cottages for two labourers and their families; the upper portion was arranged as a storehouse for divers kinds of roots and fruits.

Hardy describes it in poor condition as it was until restoration in the 1960s.

Knapwater House is Miss Aldclyffe's home:

regularly and substantially built of clear grey freestone throughout, in that plainer fashion of classicism which prevailed at the latter end of the eighteenth century, when the copyists called designers had grown weary of fantastic variations in the Roman orders.

The waterfall that keeps Cytherea awake is still visible at the east end of the lake and the 'Fane' summer-house, where she learns that Manston loves her, was also restored in 1968.

THE PATH BESIDE THE FROOM TO STINSFORD/ MELLSTOCK CHURCH

The thatched house near **Bockhampton Bridge, Bridge Cottage**, is the dormered inn where revellers carouse one Christmas Eve in the poem *The Dead Quire*. They hear the 'aerial music' of a ghostly carol:

XIX
Then did the Quick pursue the Dead
By crystal Froome that crinkles there;
And still the viewless quire ahead
*   Voiced the old holy air.*

XX
By Bank-walk wicket, brightly bleached,
It passed, and 'twixt the hedges twain,
Dogged by the living; till it reached
*   The bottom of Church Lane.*

XXI
There, at the turning, it was heard
Drawing to where the churchyard lay:
But when they followed thitherward
*   It smalled, and died away.*

A reluctant agnostic, Hardy often attended services at Stinsford to hear the lessons he remembered from his childhood; he loved the church and was bound by all the memories it held for him. The churchyard was particularly poignant as many villagers that he knew are buried here as well as those nearest to him.

The pilgrimage began at his birthplace; it ends in this quiet place, under the great yew tree, where his heart is buried with his wives, only a few feet from his parents, brother and sisters. Many people feel it to be macabre that only his heart is here, his ashes being in Poets' Corner, Westminster Abbey, however symbolic that may be. No doubt Hardy would have expressed his thoughts on this in a poem. It is definitely the right place for the Hardy Way to end; almost full circle from the birthplace, over miles of unique Hardy country preserved for ever in the novels and poems.

AFTER THE WALK

If you are surprised or disgruntled that the walk led from Max Gate to Stinsford without going into Dorchester, I hope you will accept my reasons for this omission.

It seems to me that a guided tour round Hardy's Casterbridge at the end of a two hundred mile trek might be exhausting; there is so much to see in the town. A good night's rest and a walk without a rucksack will ensure full appreciation of the many historic and Hardy places. Also, there are some very comprehensive Hardy town guides available at the Dorchester Tourist Information Centre on Antelope Walk which I recommend for this purpose.

I shall therefore limit myself to a very short list of places that I think you should definitely view if time governs your choice.

Maumbury Rings on the southern outskirts of the town. This can be reached from Weymouth Avenue, past the Market car park and the **County Constabulary**, through a small iron gate on the left. Maumbury is particularly interesting because it spans a huge chunk of local history from prehistoric times. It was firstly a Neolithic henge from the New Stone or early Bronze Age. When the Romans founded the town of Durnovaria they heightened the banks of the henge to make an amphitheatre, a place of entertainment, according to Hardy *one of the finest ... if not the very finest, remaining in Britain*. Well over a thousand years later it was used as a gun

XXII

Each headstone of the quire, each mound,
Confronted them beneath the moon;
But no more floated therearound
*   That ancient Birth-night tune.*

XXIII

There Dewy lay by the gaunt yew tree,
There Reuben and Michael, a pace behind,
And Bowman with his family
*   By the wall that the ivies bind …*

These are members of the Mellstock choir in *Under the Greenwood Tree* who follow the *embowered path beside the Froom* back to the church to drink hot mead with bread-and-cheese before finishing their carol singing.

The little lane up to the church from the riverside path is Hardy's **Moaning Hill**. As a child he attended many services at Stinsford. *Afternoon Service at Mellstock (Circa 1850)* encapsulates the wandering concentration of the captive choirboys:

On afternoons of drowsy calm
We stood in the panelled pew
Singing one-voiced a Tate-and-Brady psalm
*   To the tune of 'Cambridge New':*

We watched the elms, we watched the rooks,
The clouds upon the breeze,
Between the whiles of glancing at our books,
*   And swaying like the trees.*

So mindless were those outpourings!
Though I am not aware
That I have gained by subtle thought on things
*   Since we stood psalming there.*

At the time some of the windows were of plain glass.

Finally, to the churchyard, to take leave of Hardy and all the richness of his writing. These lines from *Friends Beyond* now include him and I hope he would have approved of them as a fitting end to this walk through Wessex with him:

William Dewy, Tranter Reuben, Farmer Ledlow late at plough,
*   Robert's kin, and John's and Ned's*
And the Squire and Lady Susan, lie in Mellstock Churchyard now!

emplacement and fort in the Civil War, when ramps were constructed. In the eighteenth century it became a grim place of execution; imagine the scene at the hanging of 19-year-old Mary Channing in 1706. The gallows stood beyond the south west corner.

Hardy chose the 'Ring' — this *melancholy, impressive and lonely* place for furtive encounters in *The Mayor of Casterbridge* and there is an evocative description of it in the novel.

Thomas Hardy's Statue near Top o'Town roundabout at the end of High West Street on the corner of Colliton Walk. By the sculptor Eric Kennington, who also created the T.E.Lawrence effigy in St Martin's Church, Wareham, the Hardy statue was unveiled in 1931 by Sir James Barrie, O.M., a friend of Hardy and a great admirer of his work. In 1920 Barrie had written in his notebook: *'T.Hardy great when political swells are dead, rotten and forgotten.'* An avenue of limes runs northwards from here, which mark the line of the Roman wall of Durnovaria.

The Dorset County Museum in the centre of the town near the junction of High West Street with South Street. Originally founded in 1845, with William Barnes as one of its secretaries, to protect Maumbury Rings and Poundbury hill-fort from encroachment by the construction of the railway, the present museum was opened in 1884 by General Pitt-Rivers, with Lord Shaftesbury as its chairman. It is an excellent museum for archaeology, natural history and geology, and has the largest collection in the world of Hardy artefacts and William Barnes memorabilia, including a reconstruction of Hardy's Max Gate study, with the original effects.

'Gone,' I call them, gone for good, that group of local hearts and heads;
Yet at mothy curfew-tide,
And at midnight when the noon-heat breathes it back from walls and leads,

They've a way of whispering to me – fellow-wight who yet abide –
In the muted, measured note
Of a ripple under archways, or a lone cave's stillicide:

'We have triumphed: this achievement turns the bane to antidote,
Unsuccesses to success,
Many thought-worn eves and morrows to a morrow free of thought.

'No more need we corn and clothing, feel of old terrestrial stress;
Chill detraction stirs no sigh;
Fear of death has even bygone us: death gave all that we possess.'

Stinsford Church where the Hardy Way and the pilgrimage end. Hardy's heart rests here in the heart of Dorset. Behind are more than two hundred miles of glorious Wessex countryside. Bridge the gap to the present by spending some time in Dorchester. Drawing: Douglas Snowdon

Hardy's statue at Colliton Walks, Dorchester – sculpted by Eric Kennington – has been the subject of much criticism. The truth is that physically he was not a prepossessing figure; a difficult thing to capture the essence of the man in stone. But what an imagination! Drawing: R.J. Dymond

BIBLIOGRAPHY

Thomas Hardy's work

Thomas Hardy's Novels and Short Stories: The New Wessex Edition, Macmillan London Ltd., 1974

The Complete Poems of Thomas Hardy Ed. James Gibson. The New Wessex Edition, Macmillan London Ltd, 1976

Thomas Hardy's Personal Writings Ed. H. Orel. University of Kansas 1966, Macmillan 1967

Hardy, Florence Emily, *The Life of Thomas Hardy, 1840-1928* Macmillan 1962, St Martin's Press 1962. (Originally published in two volumes in 1928, it is mainly in Hardy's own words as dictated to his wife.)

Biographical works

Draper, Jo. *Thomas Hardy, A life in Pictures,* The Dovecote Press, Wimborne, 1989.

Fowles, John (Ed. And introduction) and Draper, Jo (text), *Thomas Hardy's England*, Jonathan Cape, London, 1984.

Gittings, Robert. *Young Thomas Hardy*, Heinemann Educational, London, 1975.

Gittings, Robert. *The Older Hardy*, Heinemann Educational, London, 1978.

Hawkins, Desmond. *Hardy, Novelist and Poet*, David and Charles, Newton Abbot, 1976.

Kay-Robinson, Denys. *The First Mrs Thomas Hardy*, Macmillan London Ltd, 1979.

Millgate, Michael. *Thomas Hardy, A Biography*, Oxford University Press, 1982.

Topographical works

Ashley, Harry. *The Dorset Coast, History, Love and Legend*, Countryside Books, Newbury, 1992.

Boddy, Maureen and West, Jack. *Weymouth – An Illustrated History*, The Dovecote Press, 1983.

Borrett, Danielle and Stewart. *Dorchester Rediscovered*, Amberwood Publishing, 1991.

Draper, Jo. *Dorset: The Complete Guide,* The Dovecote Press, 1986.

Edwards, Anne-Marie. I*n The Steps of Thomas Hardy,* Countryside Books, Newbury, 1989.

Hawkins, Desmond. *Hardy's Wessex,* Macmillan, London, 1983.

Kay-Robinson, Denys. *The Landscape of Thomas Hardy,* Macmillan, London, 1983.

Lea, Hermann. *The Hardy Guides, A Guide to the West Country*, Volumes 1 and 2, Ed. Gregory Stevens Cox, Penguin Books, 1986.

Legg, Rodney. *Walks in Dorset's Hardy Country*, Dorset Publishing Company, Wincanton, 1988.

Legg, Rodney. *Walks in West Dorset*, Dorset Publishing Company, Wincanton , 1991.

Legg, Rodney, Dacombe, Ron and Graham, Colin, *The Dorset Walk*, Dorset Publishing Company, Milborne Port, 1984.

Pitfield, F.P. *Hardy's Wessex Locations*, Dorset Publishing Company, Wincanton, 1992.

Robertson, Martin. *Dorset to Gloucestershire*, London, H.M.S.O. , 1992.

Tarr, Roland. *National Trail Guide, South-West Coast Path Exmouth to Poole,* Aurum Press, Countryside Commission/Ordnance Survey, London, 1990.

Other sources

Series of Tour Pamphlets, The Thomas Hardy Society Ltd., Dorchester.

The Thomas Hardy Society website. www.hardysociety.org

The Thomas Hardy Year Books from 1970, Toucan Press, Guernsey.

INDEX